THE DEVELOPMENT OF THE USA 1929–2000

Steve Waugh • John Wright
Series editor: R. Paul Evans

> This material has been endorsed by Eduqas and offers high quality support for the delivery of Eduqas qualifications.
>
> While this material has been through a quality assurance process, all responsibility for the content remains with the publisher.

Although every effort has been made to ensure that website addresses are correct at time of going to press, Hodder Education cannot be held responsible for the content of any website mentioned in this book. It is sometimes possible to find a relocated web page by typing in the address of the home page for a website in the URL window of your browser.

Orders: please contact Hachette UK Distribution, Hely Hutchinson Centre, Milton Road, Didcot, Oxfordshire, OX11 7HH. Telephone: +44 (0)1235 827827. Email education@hachette.co.uk Lines are open from 9 a.m. to 5 p.m., Monday to Friday. You can also order through our website: www.hoddereducation.co.uk

ISBN: 978 1 4718 6814 6

© R. Paul Evans, Steve Waugh, John Wright 2016

First published in 2016 by
Hodder Education,
An Hachette UK Company
Carmelite House
50 Victoria Embankment
London EC4Y 0DZ

www.hoddereducation.co.uk

Impression number 10 9 8

Year   2022

All rights reserved. Apart from any use permitted under UK copyright law, no part of this publication may be reproduced or transmitted in any form or by any means, electronic or mechanical, including photocopying and recording, or held within any information storage and retrieval system, without permission in writing from the publisher or under licence from the Copyright Licensing Agency Limited. Further details of such licences (for reprographic reproduction) may be obtained from the Copyright Licensing Agency Limited, www.cla.co.uk.

Cover photo © Heritage Image Partnership Ltd/Alamy Stock Photo

Illustrations by Aptara Inc., Barking Dog Art, DC Graphic Design Ltd and Tony Randell

Typeset in India by Aptara Inc.

Printed and bound by CPI Group (UK) Ltd, Croydon, CR0 4YY

A catalogue record for this title is available from the British Library.

CONTENTS

Introduction 4

Chapter 1   Economic downturn and recovery   6

Chapter 2   The economic impact of the Second World War and post-war developments   20

Chapter 3   The issue of civil rights, 1941–70   26

Chapter 4   Political change, 1960–2000   54

Chapter 5   Social change, 1950–2000   66

Chapter 6   Cold War rivalry   80

Chapter 7   The search for world peace since 1970   94

Examination guidance 108

Glossary 115

Index 118

Acknowledgements 120

Introduction

About the Eduqas course

During this course you must study **two** components (each carrying a weighting of 50%):

Component One: Studies in Depth

This is in two parts and consists of:
- A British Depth Study
- A non-British Depth Study

Component Two: Studies in Breadth

This is in two parts and consists of:
- A Period Study
- A Thematic Study, which includes the study of an historical site

Assessment

These studies will be assessed through four examination papers:

Component One

This will consist of a two hour examination split into two papers – one hour on the British Depth Study and one hour on the non-British Depth Study. Each study will be assessed by compulsory questions focusing on the analysis and evaluation of historical sources and interpretations. There will also be questions testing second order historical concepts such as continuity, change, consequence, significance, similarity and difference.

Component Two

This will consist of a two hour examination split into two papers – 45 minutes on the Period Study and one hour 15 minutes on the Thematic Study. Each study is assessed by five compulsory questions on the Period Study paper and seven compulsory questions on the Thematic Study paper. The main focus is on second order historical concepts but there is also some testing of source analysis and evaluation skills.

About the book

This book covers the option 2A The Development of the USA, 1929–2000 which is a Period Study and is part of Component Two. The book is divided into seven chapters.

1: Economic downturn and recovery

This chapter examines the key question: *How was the USA affected by the Great Depression between 1929 and 1945?* It explains the impact of the Wall Street Crash, Republican attempts to deal with the crisis, life during the Depression, and Roosevelt and the New Deal.

2: The economic impact of the Second World War and post-war developments

This chapter examines the key question: *How had the economy of the USA changed by the 1960s?* It examines industrial output in the years after the Second World War, post-war affluence, consumerism and suburbanisation and 'poverty amidst plenty'.

3: The issue of civil rights, 1941–70

This chapter examines the key question: *Why was it difficult for black American people to gain equal rights between 1941 and 1970?* This includes the contribution of black American people to the war effort during the Second World War, the issue of education – *Brown* v. *Topeka*, Little Rock High and the Montgomery bus boycott, the roles of Martin Luther King and Malcolm X, and the civil rights legislation.

4: Political change, 1960–2000

This chapter examines the key question: *What were the main political developments in the USA between 1960 and 2000?* It explains the domestic policies of Kennedy, Nixon and Watergate, the Reagan years and changes under Bush Senior and Clinton.

5: Social change, 1950–2000

This chapter examines the key question: *How did American society change between 1950 and 2000?* and includes changes in music, entertainment, media and literature, changes in youth culture and student protest, and the changing role of women.

6: Cold War rivalry

This chapter examines the key question: *Why did relations between the USA and the USSR deteriorate between 1945 and 1973?* It examines the Truman Doctrine and containment of communism, the Berlin Crisis of 1948–49, the Cuban Missile Crisis of 1962 and US involvement in Vietnam.

7: The search for world peace since 1970

This chapter examines the key question: *What has been the USA's role in the search for peace since 1970?* It explains détente and the attempts to limit arms, changing relations with China, the fall of communism and the end of the Cold War, and US involvement in Iran, Iraq and the Gulf War.

Features

Each chapter of this book:

- contains activities – some develop the historical skills you will need, others are exam-style questions that give you the opportunity to practise exam skills
- refers you to step-by-step guidance, marked answers and advice on how to answer particular question types in the period study paper
- defines key terms and highlights glossary terms in bold and colour the first time they appear in each chapter.

Eduqas examination

COMPONENT 2: STUDIES IN BREADTH

Period Study

2A. **The Development of the USA, 1929–2000**

Time allowed: 45 minutes

1. Describe the impact of the Watergate Scandal. [5 marks]

   In Question 1 you have to demonstrate your own knowledge and understanding of a key feature. You should aim to include specific factual detail.

2. How far did the policy of détente change relations between the USA and the USSR? [6 marks]

   In Question 2 you have to make a judgement about the extent of change resulting from a particular event, movement, individual or turning point.

3. The lives of many American people changed after 1929 due to the influence of such developments as:
   - the sharp fall in share prices
   - the dramatic rise in unemployment
   - the policies of the Republican president.

   Arrange the developments in order of their significance in changing the lives of many American people after 1929. Explain your choices. [9 marks]

   In Question 3 you have to rank order three factors according to their significance to the key issue identified in the question, using your own knowledge to support your decision.

4. Explain why Malcolm X was important in the fight for civil rights during the 1960s? [8 marks]

   In Question 4 you have to provide a number of specific reasons to explain a key issue.

5. How important was the Truman Doctrine of Containment to US foreign policy between 1945 and 1973? [12 marks]

   Total marks for the paper: 40

   In Question 5 you need to use your own knowledge to debate an issue, looking at both sides of the argument. You should provide a reasoned judgement upon the set question.

1 Economic downturn and recovery

> The USA was badly affected by the Wall Street Crash of 1929. It led to the Great Depression in both the cities and the countryside, with millions of people out of work. For many, life during the Depression was difficult. People lost their homes and jobs, and family life was affected. The Republican President Herbert Hoover became increasingly unpopular as he appeared to do little to ease the effects of the economic downturn. In 1932 Hoover lost the presidential election to Franklin D. Roosevelt who introduced a New Deal to help those badly affected by the Depression. However, the New Deal was met by opposition from a variety of groups and individuals, especially the Supreme Court.

The impact of the Wall Street Crash and life during the Depression

After the First World War (1914–18), the USA experienced an economic boom and people thought that the country would prosper for many years. The policies of successive Republican presidents as well as the advanced techniques of production used by the car industry helped to further the boom. During the 1920s, more and more Americans began to invest in shares and prices kept rising. In 1928, however, shares did not rise as much as in previous years. This led to less confidence in the market and a drop in share prices. When, in the autumn of 1929, some experts started to sell their shares before their value fell even further, small investors panicked and rushed to sell their own shares.

The real panic selling began on 19 October 1929. Nearly 3.5 million shares were bought and sold and prices began to fall quickly. The following Thursday, 24 October, became known as 'Black Thursday' as nearly 13 million shares were traded and share prices collapsed. Thousands of investors lost millions of dollars and were ruined. This event became known as the Wall Street Crash – named after the street where the US stock market was based.

Unemployment

The impact of the Wall Street Crash was quite spectacular. By the end of 1929, there were about 2.5 million unemployed in the USA. This figure increased dramatically during the years 1929–32 (see Figure 1.1) due to the collapse of the US economy and a fall in world trade. Many businesses closed due to the fall in demand for American consumer goods both at home and abroad.

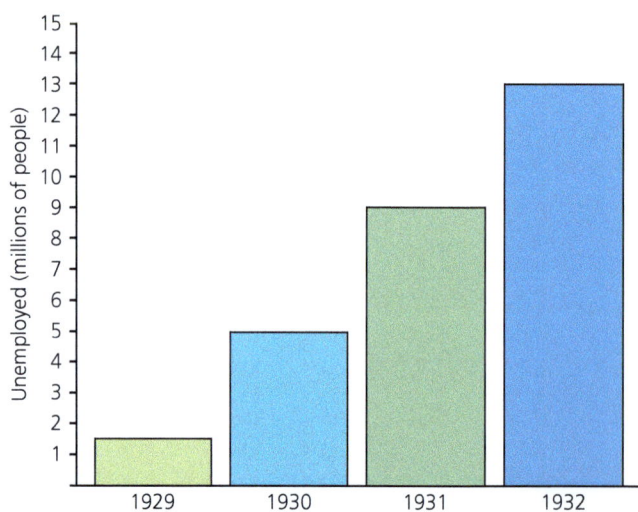
▲ Figure 1.1: The growth of unemployment, 1929–32

1 Economic downturn and recovery

Depression in the cities

The crisis gathered momentum and it was not long before factories began to close down. People stopped spending, and production had to slow down or stop. The industrial cities saw a rapid rise in unemployment and by 1933 almost one-third of the workforce was unemployed.

As people lost their jobs, they lost their homes. Some built alternative 'homes' in what became known as **Hoovervilles** (see page 8). Many of the unemployed in cities slept on the streets. Some homeless people drifted across the country seeking work, commonly referred to at the time as '**hobos**'. They caught rides on freight trains in search of work (see Source B). It was estimated that in 1932 there were more than 2 million hobos.

When the **Great Depression** began, black workers were often the first to be sacked. Unemployment amongst black people was 50 per cent by 1933, whereas it was about 20 per cent for white American people.

> **Source A:** From *Hard Times* by Studs Terkel, 1970. This extract is from an interview with a black American person who lived through the Depression
>
> *The Negro was born in depression. The Great Depression as you call it didn't mean much to him. The Depression only became official when it hit the white man.*

ACTIVITIES

1. What can you learn from Source A about the Depression?
2. What do Sources B and C show about the extent of the Depression?
3. Why was the Wall Street Crash a turning point in America's economic development?

Depression in the countryside

Bankruptcy among farmers grew because they were unable to sell their produce. In many cases, food was left to rot in the ground. The drought of 1931 compounded the farmers' problems as reduced prices and falling output meant there was no hope of breaking even financially.

Oklahoma, Colorado, New Mexico and Kansas were the states worst hit by the drought. Poor farming methods had exhausted the soil and in the drought the soil turned to dust. When the winds came the soil blew away, creating dust storms. The affected area, about 20 million hectares, became known as the 'dust bowl'.

More than 1 million people left their homes to seek work in the fruit-growing areas of the west coast. Farmers and their families packed what they could, tied it to their cars or wagons, and set off towards the west coast. Those from Oklahoma were nicknamed 'Okies' and those from Arkansas were 'Arkies'. Farmers in the west were quite happy to employ these people as they worked for very low wages. They would set up camps at the edge of towns and seek work wherever they could get it. They were often resented by locals because they were taking their jobs.

> **Source C:** From the memoir of Dorothea Lange, *The Assignment I'll Never Forget: Migrant Mothers*, 1960. Here she is describing meeting one of the migrant workers who had arrived in California
>
> *I approached the hungry woman ... She told me she was 32. She said she had been living on frozen vegetables from surrounding fields and birds that her children had killed. She had just sold the tyres from the car to buy food.*

Practice question

1. Explain why the lives of many farmers changed during the Depression.
   (For guidance, see page 112.)

◀ **Source B:** Homeless labourers by a freight train, early 1930s

Family life

The Depression had a tremendous effect on family life.

- Young people were reluctant to take on the extra commitment of marriage. Marriages fell from 1.23 million in 1929 to 982,000 in 1932. The birth rate also fell.
- The suicide rate rose dramatically from 12.6 suicides per 1,000 people in 1926 to 17.4 per 1,000 at its peak in 1932.
- In some states, such as Arkansas, schools were closed down for 10 months of the year because there was not enough money to pay teachers.
- The magazine *Fortune* estimated that by 1932 about 25 per cent of the population was receiving no income. Because there was no national system of social security, the unemployed and their dependants relied on charitable organisations such as the Red Cross.

Hoovervilles

Those American people who lost their homes as a result of becoming unemployed moved to the edges of towns and cities. They built homes of tin, wood and cardboard. These became known as Hoovervilles. There was even a Hooverville in Central Park, New York City. President Hoover was blamed for the lack of support and relief, and the sarcastic name for the dwellings soon caught on. It has been estimated that at their peak, several hundred thousand people across the USA lived in Hoovervilles.

Hoovervilles had no running water or sewage systems and were therefore a public health concern for the towns and cities in which they were built. There were frequent attempts to move the inhabitants on, but there were still Hoovervilles in existence as late as 1941, when the federal government gave powers to state and city authorities to remove them.

There were other terms, heavy with irony, which used Hoover's name:

- 'Hoover blankets' were layers of newspapers
- 'Hoover flags' were men's trouser pockets turned inside out to show they had no money
- 'Hoover wagons' were cars with horses tied to them because the owners could not afford petrol.

> **ACTIVITY**
>
> What does Source D show you about Hoovervilles?

Source D: A Hooverville in Seattle. The Hooverville existed from 1932 to 1941

1 Economic downturn and recovery

The Bonus Marchers

The Bonus Marchers were First World War veterans who had been promised a bonus for serving in the war, payable in 1945. The veterans felt that they could not wait that long to be paid. In May and June 1932, a Bonus Expeditionary Force, made up of over 12,000 unemployed and homeless veterans from all over the USA, marched to Washington DC to voice their support for a bill which would allow early payment of the bonuses.

The marchers brought their wives and children and built a Hooverville outside the capital and said they would stay there until the bonus bill was passed. Government officials labelled them a rabble. To pay the bonus to these men would have cost US$2.3 million, and President Hoover felt that it was simply too much. **Congress** did provide money to pay for transport home for the marchers, but about 5,000 refused to leave. The government labelled these men communists and sent in the police to clear them from the old buildings in which they lived. Conflict broke out and two veterans were killed.

Hoover then called in the army to control the situation. The armed forces were told to disperse the Bonus Marchers and the Hooverville was razed to the ground (see Sources E and F). More than 100 people were injured and a baby died of tear-gas poisoning. For many Americans this reinforced their conviction that Hoover did not care.

> **Source F:** From an interview with A.E. McIntyre, Federal Trade Commissioner, who witnessed the attacks on the Bonus Marchers
>
> *The Bonus Marchers were very calm. When the army appeared the Marchers started beating on tin pans and shouting 'here come our buddies'. The Bonus Marchers expected the army to be in sympathy with them. Each soldier was in full battle dress. Each had a gas mask and tear gas bombs. Soon, almost everyone disappeared from view, because tear gas bombs exploded. Flames were coming up where the soldiers had set fire to the buildings in order to drive the Marchers out.*

ACTIVITIES

1. Use Sources E and F and your own knowledge to describe how the Bonus Marchers were treated.
2. Working in pairs, produce two different sets of headlines to accompany Source E:
   - one by the government
   - one by the Bonus Marchers.

◀ **Source E:** Soldiers driving the Bonus Marchers out of Washington DC with tear gas, July 1932

Republican attempts to deal with the crisis

Herbert Hoover, the Republican Party candidate, won the 1928 presidential election and was president until March 1933. There is much controversy about Hoover's attempts to deal with the Depression. He was criticised at the time and in later years for doing too little to help those affected by the Depression. However, he did make some attempts to move towards recovery, especially in his later years as president.

Hoover's early policies

Hoover has been criticised for allowing the economic situation to worsen after 1930. He did try to follow the ideas of the Republican Party (see Figure 1.2) and was determined to balance the budget and refused to borrow money.

- Hoover kept faith with the Republican ideas of laissez-faire and rugged individualism. Rugged individualism was the belief that individuals are responsible for their own lives without help from anyone else, including the government. They should stand or fall by their own efforts.
- He met business leaders and asked them not to cut wages or production levels.
- He passed the Hawley–Smoot Tariff Act 1930. This protected US farmers by increasing import duties on foreign goods. In retaliation, other countries refused to trade with the USA.
- He assisted farmers with the Agricultural Marketing Act 1930. This act enabled the government to lend money to farmers through special marketing groups known as co-operatives, which tried to fix reasonable price levels to ensure that goods were sold at a profit by farmers.
- He set up relief agencies, for example, the President's Organisation for Unemployment Relief, which aimed to promote and co-ordinate local relief efforts.
- He cut taxes by US$130 million.
- He won approval from Congress for US$1.8 billion for new construction and repairs to roads and dams across the USA.

A voluntary deed is infinitely more precious to our national ideal and spirit than a thousand deeds poured from the Treasury.

Each industry should assist its own employees.

Economic wounds must be healed by the producers and consumers themselves.

Each community and each state should assume full responsibility for the organisation of employment and the relief of distress.

Figure 1.2: A collection of statements made by Hoover when president. These statements were part of the Republican Party's ideas

1 Economic downturn and recovery

Hoover's policies in 1932

However, with unemployment continuing to rise in 1931 and 1932, Hoover had to accept that his policies were not working. He obtained approval from Congress to introduce a series of other measures to relieve the crisis (see Table 1.1 below).

Measure	Description
Reconstruction Finance Corporation (February 1932)	Largest federal aid given – US$2 billion in loans to ailing banks, insurance companies and railroads. The corporation was designed to last only two years and would 'strengthen confidence' and stimulate industry and create jobs.
The Emergency Relief Act (ERA) (July 1932)	Provided US$300 million to state governments to help the unemployed.
Home Loan Bank Act (July 1932)	To stimulate house building and home ownership. Twelve regional banks were set up with a collective fund of US$125 million.

▲ Table 1.1: Hoover's measures to relieve the crisis, 1932

How successful were Hoover's policies?

Hoover's measures failed to pull the USA out of the Depression. He could not escape the fact that unemployment figures continued to rise. Many US citizens saw Hoover as callous and uncaring. The popular slogan of the time was 'In Hoover we trusted, now we are busted.'

However, Hoover was not a total failure.

- He had persuaded state and local city governments to expand their public works programmes and spending by US$1.5 billion.
- He began to implement policies that were later followed by his successor Roosevelt – such as helping banks and homeowners.
- During his four-year term of office federal spending on public works exceeded that of the previous 30 years. Some of the most important public works undertaken during this time included the San Francisco Bay Bridge, the Los Angeles Aqueduct and the Boulder Dam.

> **Practice question**
>
> Describe Hoover's early policies towards the Depression.
> (For guidance, see page 108.)

> **ACTIVITIES**
>
> 1. What does Figure 1.2 suggest about Hoover's policies towards the Depression?
> 2. Study the three measures introduced by Hoover in 1932 in Table 1.1. What was the purpose of each measure?
> 3. What is the message of Source G?
> 4. Draw a picture of some scales.
>   - On the left-hand side note Hoover's successes in tackling the Depression.
>   - On the right-hand side note his failures.
>
>   Use your scales to help you answer the following question.
> 5. How successful was Hoover in dealing with the problems caused by the Depression in the years 1929–32?

◀ Source G: An American cartoon from *The Nation*: an unemployed man contemplates President Hoover's optimistic assessment of the state of the country, 1932

Roosevelt and the New Deal

Roosevelt and the 1932 presidential election

In November 1932, a presidential election was fought between Herbert Hoover (Republican) and Franklin D. Roosevelt (Democrat). Roosevelt won by a landslide – only 6 of the 48 states voted for Hoover. The result was 15,759,000 votes for Hoover and 22,810,000 for Roosevelt. Roosevelt's victory was due both to the unpopularity of Hoover and his policies, and the appeal of Roosevelt and his promise of a New Deal, which Table 1.2 summarises.

Unpopularity of Hoover	Roosevelt's appeal
• Hoover and the Republicans were blamed for the Depression. • They were blamed for failing to deal with the worst effects of the Depression. • It was only a few months since the harsh treatment of the Bonus Marchers. • Hoover had nothing new to promise voters. • Relief and government schemes were too small in scope. • Banks and businesses continued to fail and confidence fell away.	• Many were impressed by the fact that Roosevelt had overcome the effects of polio, which paralysed him from the waist down, to become a successful politician. • Roosevelt created a mood of optimism to try to break the cycle of despondency. • At meetings he kept his message simple but offered a much bolder approach: *'I pledge you, I pledge myself, to a new deal for the American people.'* • This New Deal would include the creation of jobs, assistance for the unemployed and government help for both agriculture and industry.

▲ Table 1.2: Reasons for Roosevelt's victory in the presidential campaign, 1932

Source H: A Democratic election poster, 1932

ACTIVITIES

1. What is the message of Source H?
2. Design two posters for the 1932 presidential campaign, one for Hoover and one for Roosevelt.

What was Roosevelt's New Deal?

In his nomination speech Roosevelt had promised the American people a New Deal, and now that he was president it was time to deliver it.

After his inauguration, Roosevelt set to work immediately. He felt that it was his task to restore the faith that most American people had lost in their country. The aims of the New Deal are set out in Table 1.3 and were based upon the 'three Rs' – Relief, Recovery and Reform.

Relief	<ul><li>Assist in the removal of poverty.</li><li>Provide food for the starving.</li><li>Intervene to prevent people from losing homes/farms.</li></ul>
Recovery	<ul><li>Boost the economy so that people could get jobs.</li></ul>
Reform	<ul><li>Ensure that there were welfare provisions in the future to help the unemployed, old, sick, disabled and the destitute.</li></ul>

▲ Table 1.3: The aims of the New Deal

The aims of the New Deal

Roosevelt attacked the problems of the Great Depression and pushed through a huge number of government programmes that aimed to restore the shattered economy. This period, from 9 March to 16 June 1933, became known as the Hundred Days. On 12 March 1933 he joked, 'I think this could be a good time for a beer.'

The most important task at the beginning of the Hundred Days was to stem the crisis in banking. More than 2,000 banks had closed in the 12 months before he had become president. He had to restore confidence in banking.

Roosevelt closed all banks for ten days and then, on the radio, with 60 million people listening, he explained his plans. He would allow those banks with assets to re-open and those without would be closed until he and his advisers put forward a rescue programme. He assured people that money was safer in the bank than at home. When the banks re-opened, people no longer wished to withdraw their savings. This radio talk became the first of many **fireside chats** (see Source I below and Source K on page 15).

> **Source I:** From *The Roosevelt I Knew* by Frances Perkins, 1946
>
> *When he broadcast I realised how clearly his mind focused on the people listening at the other end. As he talked his head would nod and his hands would move in simple, natural, comfortable gestures. His face would smile and light up as though he was actually sitting in the front porch or the kitchen with them. People felt this and it bound them to him with affection.*

ACTIVITY

Imagine you are the governor of a state which has industrial and agricultural workers. Write a letter to President Roosevelt indicating why his proposed solutions to the Depression will help these people.

Practice question

Explain why Roosevelt's 'fireside chats' were so important. *(For guidance, see page 112.)*

The Alphabet Agencies

During the Hundred Days Roosevelt set up numerous organisations dubbed Alphabet Agencies. The most important ones are outlined in Table 1.4 below.

Agricultural Adjustment Act (AAA)	Set up to increase farm prices and farmers' incomes. To achieve this production levels would have to drop. As production fell, prices would rise and farmers would begin to recover. In other words, farmers would be paid by the government to produce less. More than 5 million pigs were killed and thousands of hectares of cotton were ploughed back into the ground. By 1936, incomes were 1.5 times higher than they had been in 1933. The Supreme Court rejected the Act in 1936.
Civilian Conservation Corps (CCC)	Set up to create jobs for the many men aged between 18–25 who were homeless labourers or living in Hoovervilles. They were offered work in conservation projects, such as planting trees to prevent soil erosion. They received food, clothing and US$1 per day. By August 1933 there were about 250,000 men in the CCC and by 1941 more than 2 million men had been granted some work with the CCC (see Source J, page 15).
Civil Works Administration (CWA)	Set up to create public jobs. By January 1934, about 4 million mainly unskilled American people were on the CWA's payroll. Some of the workers built roads. However, some of the jobs were laughed at because they included scaring birds away from buildings or sweeping leaves in parks. In 1935 the CWA was replaced by the Works Progress Administration (WPA).
Emergency Banking Act (EBA)	Set up to restore confidence in the banking system. Part of the Act prevented banks from investing savings deposits in the stock market, which was too unpredictable to guarantee the safety of those funds.
Farm Credit Administration (FCA)	Gave low-interest loans to farmers to help them pay their debts such as mortgages. Twenty per cent of farmers benefited from the scheme.
Federal Emergency Relief Administration (FERA)	Provided US$500 million for emergency relief through grants to state and local agencies. It was a temporary measure because Roosevelt did not want his opponents to think the government was just handing money out to the unemployed.
National Recovery Administration (NRA)	Set fair prices, wages and working conditions such as maximum hours and *minimum wages* (see Source L, page 15). To encourage business leaders to comply with the codes, the NRA launched a publicity campaign. It adopted as its symbol a blue eagle poster and asked people only to buy goods from businesses displaying the poster. The Act which established the NRA was removed by the Supreme Court in 1935 (see page 19).
Public Works Administration (PWA)	Spent US$3.3 billion on large-scale public works.
Reconstruction Finance Corporation (RFC)	Roosevelt pumped US$15 billion into Hoover's agency (see page 11). Banks and businesses were able to use some of the money to restart investment.
Tennessee Valley Authority (TVA)	Aimed at regenerating the Tennessee Valley region, which was one of the most depressed regions of the USA, with more than one-half the population of 2.5 million receiving emergency relief and annual flood damage of US$1.75 million.
	The TVA was responsible for creating a system of dams to generate cheap electricity and control flooding in order to attract industry to the area. It also had the power to build recreation areas, as well as to provide health and welfare facilities.
	Eventually the activities of the TVA covered seven states, an area of 104,000 km^2 with a population of 7 million people. However, there was some opposition to the TVA from farmers whose land was flooded, and some big business owners who felt that the USA was moving towards becoming a socialist state.

▲ Table 1.4: The key activities and organisations of the Hundred Days

1 Economic downturn and recovery

▲ **Source J:** A photograph taken in 1933 showing workers in the Civilian Conservation Corps (CCC)

▲ **Source K:** A cartoon published in a 1933 newspaper: 'The Spirit of the New Deal'. Roosevelt is seen as the worker and businessman beneath the arms of Uncle Sam, the symbol of the USA

Source L: From one of Roosevelt's fireside chats, June 1933. Here he is talking about employers' fair wages

If all employers in each competitive group agree to pay their workers the same reasonable wages – and require the same hours – reasonable hours – then higher wages will hurt no employer. Such action is better for the employer than unemployment and low wages, because it makes more buyers for his product. That is the simple idea which is at the very heart of the Industrial Recovery Act.

Practice question

How important was the first Hundred Days in helping America recover from the effects of the Depression? *(For guidance, see pages 113–14.)*

ACTIVITIES

1. Using the information in Table 1.4 divide the alphabet agencies into three groups: 1 Relief, 2 Recovery, 3 Reform. What do you notice about your decisions?
2. What does Source J show you about the CCC?
3. Use Sources K and L and your own knowledge to explain how Roosevelt helped industry.

The second New Deal

By the end of 1934 there were still 10 million American people out of work. In January 1935, in his yearly message to Congress, Roosevelt introduced his second New Deal, a broad programme of reform to help farmers, workers, the poor and the unemployed.

The Works Progress Administration (WPA)

This was headed by Harry Hopkins (who had previously been in charge of FERA, see Table 1.4 on page 14) who was quick to put the programme into action. The mainstay of the programme was funding and building projects, including hospitals, schools, airports and harbours, thus creating employment. It:

- organised a US$4.8 billion relief programme
- put unemployed teachers back to work
- created community service schemes to employ artists, writers and actors.

Roosevelt described the work of the WPA as 'priming the pump' – in other words, the government was acting by re-starting the machinery of the economy.

The National Labour Relations Act (The Wagner Act)

Roosevelt was keen to protect the rights of workers. The Wagner Act upheld the right of workers to organise and enter into collective bargaining. The number of labour union members increased from 3 million in 1933 to 9 million in 1939. The Act also set up the National Relations Board, which was given the power to act against employers who used unfair practices, such as sacking workers who had joined the union.

◀ Source M: A cartoon from 1935: 'Roosevelt the friend of the poor'

Fair Labour Standards Act

Under the Fair Labour Standards Act:

- minimum wages and maximum hours were established for all employees of business engaged in interstate commerce
- 300,000 workers secured higher wages as a result and more than 1 million had a shorter working week
- child labour was not permitted except on farms.

Social Security Act

The Social Security Act was perhaps the most important reform of the second New Deal. By passing this Act the government at last accepted full responsibility for meeting the basic needs of its citizens. The Act established:

- pension benefits for the elderly, the orphaned and those injured in industrial accidents
- unemployment benefits funded by a tax on the payrolls of employers.

ACTIVITY

What does Source M show you about the second New Deal?

How successful was the New Deal?

The New Deal achieved a number of successes but also had failures and shortcomings.

Role of government and the president

1. The New Deal restored the faith of people in government after the laissez-faire approach of Hoover.
2. It preserved democracy and ensured there was no mass support of right-wing politicians.
3. It greatly extended the role of central government and the president.
4. Roosevelt gave too much power to the federal government and the presidency. The federal government was becoming directly involved in areas which had traditionally been managed by state governments.

Economy

1. The New Deal stabilised the US banking system and cut the number of business failures.
2. It provided only short-term solutions and did not solve the underlying economic problems.
3. It greatly improved the infrastructure of the USA by providing roads, schools and power stations.
4. The US economy took longer to recover than that of most European countries. When, in 1937, Roosevelt reduced the New Deal budget, the country went back into depression.

Unemployment and industrial workers

1. The Alphabet Agencies provided only short-term jobs. Once these ended, people were back on the dole. Even at its best in 1937, there were still over 14 million out of work. It was the Second World War that brought an end to unemployment.
2. The Alphabet Agencies provided work for millions: unemployment fell from a peak of 24.9 million in 1933 to 14.3 million four years later.
3. The NRA and the second New Deal greatly strengthened the position of labour unions and made corporations negotiate with them.
4. Unions were still treated with great suspicion by employers. Indeed, many strikes were broken up with brutal violence in the 1930s.

Social welfare

1. The Social Security Act provided the USA with a semi-welfare state which included pensions for the elderly and widows and state help for the sick and disabled.
2. Some argued that social welfare measures put too much pressure on taxpayers and encouraged people to 'sponge' off the state.

Black Americans

1. Many New Deal agencies discriminated against black people. They were either given no work, or received worse treatment or lower wages than their white colleagues.
2. Around 200,000 black American people received benefits from the CCC (see page 14) and other New Deal agencies. Many benefited from slum clearance programmes and housing projects.
3. Roosevelt did little to end segregation and discrimination in the Deep South.

Women

1. Some state governments tried to avoid social security payments to women by introducing special qualifications.
2. Some women achieved prominent positions in the New Deal. Eleanor Roosevelt became an important campaigner for social reform. Frances Perkins (see Source I, page 13) was the first woman to be appointed to a cabinet post as Secretary of Labour.
3. Some of the National Industry Recovery Act codes of 1933 actually required women to be paid less than men.
4. Only 8,000 women were employed by the CCC out of the 2.75 million people involved in it.

> **ACTIVITIES**
>
> 1. Organise the statements on this page into successes and failures of the New Deal.
> 2. How successful was the New Deal?

Opposition to the New Deal

The New Deal drew opposition from a number of individuals and groups as well as the Supreme Court.

Individuals

The New Deal was criticised by individuals who believed that Roosevelt was not doing enough. They had their own ideas about what he should be doing.

- Huey Long had been governor of the State of Louisiana. He claimed that Roosevelt failed to share out the nation's wealth fairly and announced his own plans to do this under the slogan 'Share Our Wealth'. Long attracted much support but was killed by a doctor whose career he had ruined.
- Catholic priest Father Charles Coughlin criticised the New Deal for not doing enough and labelled Roosevelt as 'anti-God' because he was not really helping the needy. Father Coughlin's main influence came from his weekly radio broadcasts which attracted over 40 million listeners.
- Dr Frances Townsend, former army doctor and old-age activist, gained much support from the elderly who, by 1934, had benefited little from the New Deal. He set up an organisation called 'Old Age Revolving Pension Plan', also known as the Townsend clubs, which had attracted 5 million members by 1935.

Opposition from politicians

Roosevelt also faced opposition from a variety of political groups.

- The Republicans were strong opponents of the New Deal (see Source N). Not only were they traditional opponents of the Democrats, the Republicans were also the party which represented the interests of America's rich families and large business corporations. These people believed that Roosevelt was doing too much to help people and was changing the accepted role of government in the USA.
- The American Liberty League was set up in 1934 to preserve individual freedom and was backed by wealthy businessmen; two of these, Alfred Smith and John Davis, rather surprisingly had previously stood as Democrat presidential candidates. The League believed that the New Deal threatened the Constitution of the USA and the freedom of the individual.
- Even some members of Roosevelt's own party, the Democrats, opposed the New Deal. They were known as Conservative Democrats, many of whom came from the South and represented farming areas. They were especially against the Wagner Act (see page 16) which had given greater powers to the trade unions.

> **Source N:** From a 1936 manifesto for the Republican Party
>
> *America is in peril. For three long years the New Deal administration has dishonoured the American traditions and betrayed the pledges upon which the Democratic Party sought and received public support. The rights and liberties of American citizens have been violated. It has created a vast multitude of new offices, filled them with its favourites, set up a centralised bureaucracy and sent out swarms of inspectors to harass our people.*

The Supreme Court

One reason that the Supreme Court opposed some of Roosevelt's measures was that the court was dominated by Republican judges. Between 1861 and 1933 there had been only 16 years of Democrat presidents and therefore few opportunities to nominate Democrat judges.

Out of the 16 cases concerning the Alphabet Agencies which were tried by the Supreme Court in 1935 and 1936, the judges declared that, in 11 cases, Roosevelt had acted unconstitutionally. In reality, he was using central or federal powers which the Constitution had not given him. The two cases on page 19 show the opposition he faced.

The 'Sick Chickens' case, 1935

This involved four brothers, the Schechters, who ran a poultry business. In 1933 they signed the rules of the National Recovery Administration (NRA) which had been set up by the National Industrial Recovery Act (NIRA). These rules governed fair prices, wages and competition. In 1935, the NRA took them to court for selling a batch of diseased chickens unfit for human consumption. The Schechters appealed to the Supreme Court which declared the NIRA illegal because its activities were unconstitutional. It gave the federal government powers that it should not have to interfere in state affairs, in this case the state of New York. As a result, 750 of the NRA codes of practice were immediately scrapped.

US v. *Butler*, 1936

In this case the Supreme Court declared the Agricultural Adjustment Act illegal. The judges decided that giving help to farmers was a matter for each state government, not the federal government. As a result all help to farmers ceased.

Roosevelt's attempts at reform

After his massive victory in the 1936 presidential election, Roosevelt decided that public opinion was behind his New Deal. Therefore, in February 1937, he threatened to retire those judges in the Supreme Court who were over 70, and replace them with younger ones who supported his policies.

These attempts failed for two reasons. First, many saw this as unconstitutional, believing the president to be trying to destroy the position of the Supreme Court by packing it with his own supporters. Second, Roosevelt failed to consult senior members of his own party and many Conservative Democrats opposed his reform.

Nevertheless, in March and April 1937 the Supreme Court reversed the 'Sick Chickens' decision and accepted his Social Security Act which brought in old-age pensions and unemployment insurance (see page 16). Nonetheless, the whole episode had damaged Roosevelt's reputation and lost him the support of some members of his own party.

> ### ACTIVITIES
> 1. What does Source O show you about Roosevelt's relationship with the Supreme Court?
> 2. Put together your own mind map showing the reasons why there was opposition to the New Deal. Place your reasons in rank order clockwise, beginning with the most important reason at the top.
> 3. How successful was opposition to the New Deal?

> ### Practice questions
> 1. Explain why many Republicans opposed the New Deal. *(For guidance, see page 112.)*
> 2. How far did the rulings of the Supreme Court limit the New Deal? *(For guidance, see page 109.)*

THE LINE OF LEAST RESISTANCE

▲ **Source O:** A cartoon of 1936 showing Roosevelt lassoing a Supreme Court judge

2 The economic impact of the Second World War and post-war developments

On 7 December 1941, Japan launched an attack on the American fleet at Pearl Harbor. Within four days the USA was at war with Japan and Germany. The Second World War brought about important economic changes. America's involvement in the war meant that industry became geared to war production. The Depression was finally ended and the grinding poverty of the 1930s disappeared. By 1945, there were more jobs than applicants. Though there was rationing, there was affluence because of full employment, and after the war people found they had large amounts of disposable income to spend on consumer goods.

Industrial output

As the US economy began to improve after 1939, it became clear that for industrial output to increase, new factories would have to be built and existing ones re-equipped. This meant relying on the expertise of **industrialists** of the day.

Big business and the war effort

Roosevelt was determined to make use of leading US businessmen to provide for the needs of war. The War Production Board was run by a leading industrialist, while another important industrialist, Henry J. Kaiser, had been heavily involved in the Tennessee Valley Authority. Roosevelt called in other industrialists to ask their advice on meeting the demands of wartime production and setting targets, allowing them to decide which companies would produce particular goods. For example, **General Motors** produced heavy machine guns and thousands of other war products. Indeed, the vast majority of contracts went to larger firms. In return, the firms made a lot of money.

The effects of the war on the US economy

The Second World War enabled the USA to expand its industrial and military complexes on a huge scale and, by September 1945, it emerged as the most powerful economy in the world. The war gave the USA immense advantages over both its allies and its enemies. The dark days of the Great Depression became a distant memory and the USA became a country where there were always lots of jobs available. Fears of a return to the 1930s soon evaporated when the USA experienced phenomenal economic growth in the post-war years. During the war, US industry was able to expand as a result of the Lend Lease programme to its allies whereby huge amounts of aid were given to Britain, the **USSR** and Latin America. By 1960, the USA was the strongest economic power in the world.

The workforce

As a result of **conscription** (compulsory military service) about 16 million American men and women served in the US armed forces. This meant that many more workers were needed on the home front. This, in turn, put an end to the serious problem of unemployment caused by the Depression. In 1939, unemployment stood at 9.5 million. By 1944, it had fallen to 670,000. Fourteen million people worked in the factories. For example, General Motors took on an extra 750,000 workers during the war. Nearly 4 million workers, many of these black American people, **migrated** from the rural South to the industrial North. Table 2.1 (page 21) illustrates the impact of the war on unemployment.

2 The economic impact of the Second World War and post-war developments

Probably the greatest change was in the employment of women. Although there were already 12 million working women in the USA, a further 7 million joined the workforce, taking on jobs from which they had previously been excluded. For example, one in three aircraft workers were women, and half of those working in electronics and munitions were also women.

		1940	1941	1942	1943	1944	1945
Civilian labour force	Total	55.6	55.91	56.4	55.5	54.6	53.8
Unemployed	Total	8.1	5.5	2.6	1.07	0.6	1.04
	Percentage of labour force	14.6	9.9	4.7	1.9	1.2	1.9

▲ Table 2.1: Civilian unemployment during the Second World War (numbers in millions)

Increasing industrial production

The USA became the arsenal of the Allied powers. Roosevelt believed that to win a modern war you had to have more of everything than your opponents. Traditional industries such as coal, iron, steel and oil greatly expanded due to government contracts. After the Japanese attack on Pearl Harbor, Roosevelt created the War Production Board (WPB) and its main aim was to increase US war production. By 1944 the USA was producing almost one-half of the weapons in the world. The success of the government organisations in increasing wartime production can be seen in Table 2.2.

	1940	1941	1942	1943	1944
Aircraft	245	630	1706	2842	2805
Munitions	140	423	2167	3803	2033
Shipbuilding	159	375	1091	1815	1710
Aluminium	126	189	318	561	474
Rubber	109	144	152	202	206
Steel	131	171	190	202	197

▲ Table 2.2: Indices of US manufacturing output (1939 = 100)

The scale of US production

Any fears that senior politicians had at the beginning of the war about the USA's ability to produce military hardware on an industrial scale proved to be unfounded (Source A). The industrial boom of the period before the Depression was duplicated and in 1945, at the end of the war, it was clear that the scale of US industrial output had been immense. Private companies had applied their peacetime approach to business and had shown that they could meet the demands of total war with ease. For example:

- by 1944, 25 per cent of Britain's military equipment was produced by the USA
- by 1945, 50 per cent of the world's manufacturing took place in the USA
- the US gross national product grew from about US$200,000 million in 1940 to US$300,000 million in 1950.

> **Source A:** From the diary of Henry Stimson, the US Secretary of War, 1941
>
> *If we are going to war in a capitalist country we've got to let business make money out of the process or business doesn't work.*

ACTIVITIES

1. What can you learn from Table 2.1 about unemployment in the USA in the years 1940–45?
2. What does Table 2.2 indicate about US wartime production?
3. Study Source A. What incentive to business is suggested by Stimson?

Practice question

Explain why unemployment fell during the war years. *(For guidance, see page 112.)*

US industry after the Second World War

Importantly, the American domestic market proved to be much more buoyant than had been anticipated. The millions of US citizens who had purchased war **bonds** (see Source B) now began to cash them in and this amounted to almost US$200 billion. Ordinary American people wanted to leave rationing behind and buy consumer goods. The automobile industry dominated by the 'Big Three' – Ford, General Motors and Chrysler – boomed again. Sales of new cars rose from 69,500 in 1945 to 6.7 million by 1950. There was also a surge in house building, which was stimulated by low interest rates for returning servicemen.

Military spending

Moreover, as the **Cold War** developed after 1948, the rise in defence spending helped sustain the economic boom. In 1948, the US defence budget was about US$11 billion. In the 1950s, defence spending was between US$40 and US$50 billion per year. Billions of dollars were spent on weapons research and development. Desert areas in Arizona and New Mexico became centres for weapons testing. Many firms followed the military to their new bases, being awarded lucrative contracts to provide weapons, research and equipment. California, in particular, benefited from military contracts and one of the knock-on effects was the development of an industry in high technology that was to see it become the centre of the computer industry.

Open trading

Importantly, world markets began to open up now that the seas were free and demand for consumer goods began to rise. The US anticipated that there would be an open trading system in which there were no tariffs or trading restrictions. Because US industry had not been damaged by air attacks, it meant that the US had a clear advantage over the European countries that had been ravaged and devastated by war. Demand from Europe and other markets helped to keep US production high.

Industry and economic expansion

Economic expansion created greater employment opportunities in many industries, for example, aircraft production, chemicals and electrical goods. As consumer tastes changed, the processed food industry made huge gains. Tobacco companies also made vast profits and employed many people. By the end of the 1940s, the USA produced one-half of the world's manufactured goods: 57 per cent of steel, 62 per cent of oil and 80 per cent of cars.

> **Interpretation 1:** An excerpt from *War, Economy, and Society, 1939-1945*, by A. Milward, published in 1979
>
> *The United States emerged in 1945 in an incomparably stronger position economically than in 1941 ... By 1945, the foundations of the United States' economic domination over the next quarter of a century had been secured ... [This] may have been the most influential consequence of the Second World War for the post-war world.*

ACTIVITIES

1. What does Source B show you about government bonds?
2. Was the Second World War a turning point in the recovery of the US economy?

Source B: A US government poster advertising war bonds, December 1941. The slogan reads, 'Buy Defense bonds and stamps now'

2 The economic impact of the Second World War and post-war developments

Post-war affluence, consumerism and suburbanisation

Affluence and consumerism

After President Roosevelt's unexpected death on 12 April 1945, Vice President Harry Truman was sworn in as the new president. He introduced a programme of economic development and social welfare which became known as the Fair Deal. In his 1949 State of the Union Address to Congress, Truman stated that 'Every segment of our population, and every individual, has a right to expect from his government a fair deal.' This policy was continued by his successor, Eisenhower, and led to the prosperity of the 1950s. The statistics in Table 2.3 seem to suggest an affluent society getting richer.

There were several reasons for this.

- American people spent US$100 billion they had saved during the Second World War. Much of this money went on consumer goods, especially televisions and cars.
- Hire purchase, known as consumer credit, increased by 800 per cent between 1945 and 1957.
- The improved efficiency of the workforce meant that consumer goods could be produced more cheaply, which kept down prices.
- The growth in population (see page 24) also provided a greater demand for goods.

	Cars	Televisions	Refrigerators	Washing machines
1950	60.0	26.4	86.4	71.9
1956	73.0	81.0	96.0	86.8

▲ Table 2.3: Consumer goods ownership in 1950 and 1956 (%)

- Finally, the Korean War (1950–53) and the ongoing Cold War meant that US industry was kept busy turning out new weapons, which led to big orders for industries such as steel, coal and electronics.

In 1960, the standard of living of the average American person was three times that of the average British person. They were encouraged to spend and shopping became a popular recreational activity. The average wages of factory workers went up from US$55 per week in 1950 to US$80 in 1959.

In new homes, all the modern conveniences were expected and became necessities not luxuries (Source C). Movies and magazines carried the news of American success to millions of envious people around the world. Vast supermarkets, new freeways, large cars with fins and chrome (Source D), and television games were all, it was claimed, symbols of a flourishing economy and a free society.

The invention of the transistor, which replaced large and costly valves in such things as radios and televisions, revolutionised the manufacture of electric circuits and by 1960, 90 per cent of homes had television sets, which changed the pattern of daily life.

> **Source C:** From William E. Leuchtenberg, *A Troubled Feast, American Society Since 1945*, published in 1973
>
> *When the Paris Editor of the 'U.S. News and World Report' came home to the United States in 1960 after twelve years abroad, he was astonished at the changes. He had been living in France where only one family in ten had a bath tub with hot running water and was coming home to a country where, in some sections of California, at least one family in ten owned a swimming pool. With larger incomes than ever before there were, for consumers, shopping precincts with piped music, and supermarkets with row upon row of brilliantly coloured cartons.*

ACTIVITY

What do Sources C and D reveal about consumerism in the 1950s?

Practice question

Explain why US society became more affluent during the 1950s and 1960s.
(For guidance, see page 112.)

▲ **Source D:** An advertisement from 1957 for the Pontiac motor car

Practice questions

1. Describe the main features of life in suburbia in the 1950s. *(For guidance, see page 108.)*
2. Explain why people moved to the suburbs in the 1950s. *(For guidance, see page 112.)*

ACTIVITY

Study Source E. What disadvantages were there in living in such a suburban development?

Suburbanisation

Suburbia was a new development in the late 1940s and 1950s. Many middle-class families abandoned the centre of cities and moved to new homes in the suburbs. The first planned suburb was Levittown on Long Island, about 45 km from Manhattan (Source E). The suburbanisation of the USA was a central part of the campaign to create the 'ideal' American family, and the federal government played a direct role in the mass migration from the cities. This movement was due to several factors.

- Suburbia embodied the 'American Dream' for many young couples in post-war America as a place where they could own their own home and raise their children away from the dangers of city life.
- Houses were reasonably priced and were made affordable to newly married middle-class couples through low-interest mortgages.
- Most families had at least one car, which meant that people no longer had to live close to their place of work.
- The economic growth and affluence of the post-war years made these new houses and consumer goods affordable to an increasing number of American people.
- Between 1945 and 1960, a **baby boom** increased the population by about 40 million and increased the demand for new homes. The number of home owners increased from 23,600,000 in 1950 to 32,800,00 in 1960.

By 1960 over 20 per cent of American families lived in homes that had been built in the 1950s. These homes included all the 'mod-cons', such as televisions, washing machines and fridges. Owning a car or the latest hi-fi record player, or perhaps installing a swimming pool, became important status symbols in suburbia.

However, many women who were unable to go out to work felt isolated and bored in their new suburban homes and looked for companionship. Co-operation and group participation helped to forge community spirit, for example, women organised **Tupperware parties** where they met over coffee to buy kitchen products.

Though houses were affordable, not everyone had the opportunity to buy a suburban home. Many building developers refused to sell homes to ethnic minority groups. In 1960, when Levittown had a population of 65,000, there was not one dwelling owned by an African-American person.

▼ Source E: Aerial photograph of Levittown, a suburb of New York, April 1949

Poverty in the midst of plenty

Not every American person shared in this new-found affluence.

- Many American people, including black Americans, remained part of an underclass that was unable to share in the prosperity. In 1959, 29 per cent of the population lived below the poverty line (Source F).
- People's income was also affected by the area in which they lived. People in the southern states, in particular, remained well behind those of the north or the west coast.
- In 1955, 40 per cent of New York's recipients of welfare were African-American people.
- There was no national health service and the cost of medical care rose very rapidly. The USA lagged behind many European countries in providing good pensions and welfare services (Source G).

Source G: Part of a speech by Adlai Stevenson, a Democrat senator, in 1952

How can we talk about prosperity to the sick who cannot afford proper medical care? How can we talk about prosperity to the hundreds of thousands who can find no decent place to live at prices they can afford? And how can we talk about prosperity to a sharecropper living on worn-out land, or to city dwellers packed six to a room in a unit tenement with a garbage-strewn alley for their children's playground? To these people, national prosperity is a mockery – to the 11 million families in this nation with incomes of less than $2,000 a year.

Source H: From *The Other America: Poverty in the United States* written in 1962, by Michael Harrington. This book was said to have influenced Presidents Kennedy and Johnson in their domestic reform programmes

The poor live in a culture of poverty ... [and] for reasons beyond their control, cannot help themselves ... The poor get sick more than anyone else in society ... When they become sick, they are sick longer than any other group in society. Because they are sick more often and longer than anyone else, they lose wages and work, and find it difficult to hold a steady job. And because of this, they cannot pay for good housing, for a nutritious diet, for doctors ... and their prospect is to move to an even lower level ... toward even more suffering.

ACTIVITIES

1. Suggest reasons why Source F was published in newspapers across the USA.
2. Study Source G. Why was it significant that a senator made this speech?
3. Study Source H. Suggest reasons why Presidents Kennedy and Johnson were influenced by the book.

Practice question

Explain why some American people did not experience the new-found affluence of the 1950s. *(For guidance see page 112.)*

Source F: Photograph of slum tenements, Chicago 1950

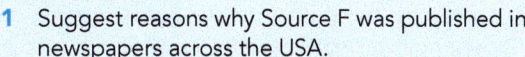

3 The issue of civil rights, 1941–70

Throughout the 1920s and 1930s there was a great deal of racial hatred and inequality towards many black American people. Discrimination continued in the 1940s, and despite the contribution of black American people to the war effort their position had improved little by the end of the Second World War. However, there was considerable progress in the search for improved civil rights during the 1950s and 1960s. In education, landmark cases such as *Brown* v. *Topeka* and events at Little Rock High did remove segregation but there was often unwillingness on the part of many states to embrace the changes. There was progress in desegregating transport after the Montgomery bus boycott and the freedom rides. Figures such as Martin Luther King and Malcolm X put the issue of civil rights at the forefront of US domestic politics and in the mid-1960s there were several pieces of legislation which aimed to ensure equality for black American people. However, by the end of the 1960s, America had seen the civil rights movement change from a peaceful, non-violent organisation to one which was populated by radical gun-carrying socialists who had shoot-outs with the police.

The contribution of black American people to the war effort

The Second World War highlighted the racism and discrimination that existed in the USA and its armed forces. This was a clear paradox because the USA was fighting against a racist regime, Nazi Germany. When war broke out, there was increased optimism that things would change for black American people, but little changed during the war (Sources A and B).

Many black American people enlisted and formed the Jim Crow army. They were aware that they would have to serve in segregated units. It was only towards the end of the war that black servicemen saw much action. By 1945, there were almost three-quarters of a million black American people in the US army and hundreds of officers.

- Black soldiers stationed in Britain were treated far better than back home. In the army, there were solely black American units with white officers.
- Before 1944, black soldiers were not allowed into combat in the Marines.
- Black people were employed as cooks and labourers or to transport supplies.
- Many black women served in the armed forces as nurses but were only allowed to treat black soldiers.
- The US Air Force would not accept black pilots. In each armed service, black American people performed the menial tasks and found promotion difficult.
- When black soldiers were injured, only blood from black soldiers could be used in their treatment; many white people felt that to mix blood would weaken the USA.
- Discrimination was worst in the navy, with black soldiers given the most dangerous job of loading ammunition onto ships bound for war zones. For example, in 1944 a horrific accident killed 323 people – most of them black sailors.
- The Tuskegee airmen (332nd Fighter Group – all black American pilots) won great acclaim acting as fighter escorts for US bombers.
- The 761st Tank Battalion also won acclaim in the Battle of the Bulge and received praise from General Patton. The battalion's nickname was the 'Black Panthers'.

3 The issue of civil rights, 1941–70

Source A: From a letter written in April 1944 by Corporal Rupert Timmingham to the magazine *Yank* about travelling in Texas with other black soldiers

We could not purchase a cup of coffee at a Texas railroad depot but the lunchroom manager said we black GIs could go on around the back to the kitchen for a sandwich and coffee. As we did, about two dozen German prisoners of war, with two American guards, came to the station. They entered the lunchroom, sat at the tables, had their meals served, talked and smoked. I stood on the outside looking on, and I could not help but ask myself why are they treated better than we are? Why are we pushed round like cattle? If we are fighting for the same thing, if we are to die for our country, then why does the Government allow such things to go on?

Source B: This 'prayer' appeared in a black newspaper in January 1943

Draftee's prayer

Dear Lord, today	Dear Lord, I'll fight,
I go to war:	I do not fear
To fight, to die	Germans or Japs,
Tell me what for	My fears are here.
	America.

Progress

Some progress was evident; for example, the US Supreme Commander, General Eisenhower, supported integrated combat units. By the end of 1944, black soldiers were fighting in these units (as seen during the Battle of the Bulge) and there were hundreds of black officers in the army and the Marines. There were also fighter squadrons of black pilots, although they were not allowed to fly in the same groups as white pilots and by the end of 1945 some 600 black pilots had been trained. By the end of the war, 58 black sailors, out of a force of almost 3.5 million, had risen to the rank of officer.

Desegregation in the navy came in 1946 and the other services in 1948. By 1955, the army had changed from being one of the most segregated organisations in the country to the most successfully integrated.

Source D: From *Citizen Soldiers* by Stephen Ambrose, 1997

The US army's chief historian concluded his wartime report in 1946 on the employment of Negro troops with these words: 'My ultimate hope is that in the long run it will be possible to assign individual Negro soldiers and officers to any unit in the Army where they are qualified as individuals to serve efficiently.'

ACTIVITIES

1. What does Source A tell you about the treatment of black American soldiers during the Second World War?
2. What message is the writer trying to put over in Source B?
3. Use Sources C and D and your own knowledge to explain why the treatment of black American soldiers had changed by the late 1940s.

Practice question

Describe the contribution of black American people to the US armed forces during the Second World War. *(For guidance, see page 108.)*

◀ **Source C:** Black American soldiers in 1944, during the Second World War

Employment and black American people during the Second World War

As more and more men were conscripted, job opportunities in factories for black American women and older black American men increased. Despite the valuable contribution these people made they were often treated poorly. A newspaper, the *Pittsburgh Courier*, created the 'Double V' campaign after readers began commenting on the second-class status of black workers during wartime. 'Double V' meant victory at home in terms of improved civil rights as well as victory abroad against fascism on the battlefield.

In 1941, A. Philip Randolph, a leading black American activist, sought to remove discrimination in the armed forces and the workplace. He organised a 'March on Washington' movement. President Roosevelt feared the possible consequences of the march and met Randolph to discuss the issues. Roosevelt issued Executive Order 8802, which stopped discrimination in industrial and government jobs, and also set up the Fair Employment Practices Commission (FEPC). The FEPC could not force companies to employ black people, but it could use the threat of withdrawing government contracts to encourage them to do so.

During the war, over 400,000 black American people migrated from the South to the USA's industrial centres. The number of black American people employed in government service rose from 50,000 to 200,000 and by the end of the war there were more than 2 million black American people involved in industry. The war also meant a broadening of opportunities for black American women. Many became nurses but were only permitted to care for black American soldiers.

By the end of the war, the number of jobs held by black American people was at an all-time high. They accounted for 8 per cent of defence-industry jobs whereas before the war they had held only 3 per cent. The government employed 200,000 black American people, more than three times the number before the war. Black workers generally only earned one-half of what white workers earned. Trade union involvement increased and black membership rose from 15,000 in 1935 to 1.25 million in 1945.

> **Source E:** From *Mr Black Labour* by the historian D. Davis, 1972, quoting the president of the North American Aviation Company in 1942
>
> *While we are in complete sympathy with the Negro, it is against company policy to employ them as aircraft workers or mechanics, regardless of their training, but there will be some jobs as janitors [caretakers] for Negroes.*

ACTIVITIES

1. What does Source E tell you about race relations in the USA during the Second World War? *(For guidance on how to answer this type of question, see page 108.)*
2. Did the Second World War improve employment opportunities for black American people? Copy the table below and complete the boxes, explaining your answers.

Yes, because …	No, because …

▲ **Source F:** Two female workers in the arms industry during the war

The Second World War and civil rights

The Second World War period had seen some progress for black American people in employment and in the armed forces, and many black American people had become more active in campaigning for civil rights. However, discrimination and segregation remained a way of life in the southern states, while the migration of many black American people to the industrial cities of the North had created greater racial tension.

This increase in racial tension led to race riots in 47 cities. The worst of these was in Detroit in June 1943 when 25 black people and 9 white people were killed. More than 700 people were injured and there was US$2 million worth of damage done to property (Source G). In the same year, nine black American people were killed in riots in Harlem, New York. There were also riots at nine black army training camps, where the soldiers resented their unequal treatment.

Awareness of discrimination and its injustice led to a growth in the membership of the National Association for the Advancement of Coloured People (NAACP) during the war – from 50,000 to 450,000. Many of the new members were professionals, but there were also many new urban workers.

A new organisation called the Congress of Racial Equality (CORE) was founded by James Farmer in 1942. CORE was inspired by the non-violent tactics of Mahatma Gandhi in India. It used the idea of sit-ins at cinemas and restaurants; this did lead to the end of segregation in some northern cities. There was increased interest in politics in the South among black American people and the numbers of registered voters rose from 3 per cent in 1940 to 12 per cent in 1947.

The issue of civil rights split the Democrats in the 1948 presidential election. Truman wanted to introduce a civil rights bill (which would ban poll taxes) and also proposed an anti-lynching bill, which the Dixiecrats (southern Democratic Party politicians) rejected.

◀ **Source G:** An incident during the Detroit riots, June 1943. A black American person is trying to run away from white rioters who had just assaulted him. The man on the left is a photographer

The situation by the end of the 1940s

President Truman's 'Fair Deal' programme had offered hope, but by the end of the 1940s only modest gains had been made by those seeking improved civil rights. Truman set up a Committee on Civil Rights in 1946, and though it recommended laws to prevent lynching, a permanent commission on civil rights and the prevention of segregation in housing, nothing was done. Republicans and the Dixiecrats (see page 29) continued to block reforms. The most important reform came when the armed forces were desegregated in 1948 (Source H).

Nevertheless, because of their contribution during the war, black American people were now better placed to demand their full rights as American citizens. Their plight was constantly recognised by President Truman (Source I) who made countless speeches, and though no new laws were introduced, he did raise the nation's awareness of the problems of civil rights.

> **Source H:** From Executive Order 9981, 26 July 1948
>
> *It is hereby declared to be the policy of the President that there shall be equality of treatment and opportunity for all persons in the armed services without regard to race, colour, religion, or national origin. This policy shall be put into effect as rapidly as possible, having due regard to the time required to effectuate any necessary changes without impairing efficiency or morale.*

The confidence of the NAACP was sufficiently high by the late 1940s that it felt able to challenge some states about the education of black students. The NAACP was able to show that in some states students in white schools had more money spent on them than students in black schools. This eventually led to the key case of *Brown* v. *Board of Education of Topeka* in 1954 (see page 31). There was also some improvement in voter registration for black American people in the 1940s. In 1940, 2 per cent of black American people were registered to vote, and by 1947, this had risen to 12 per cent.

> **Source I:** From a letter by Harry S. Truman, 18 August 1948, describing his revulsion at lynching
>
> *The main difficulty with the South is that they are living eighty years behind the times and the sooner they come out of it the better it will be for the country and themselves. I am asking for equality of opportunity for all human beings and, as long as I stay here, I am going to continue that fight. When the mob gangs can take four people and shoot them in the back and everybody in the country is acquainted with who did the shooting and nothing is done about it, that country is in a pretty bad fix …*

ACTIVITIES

1. Use Sources G (page 29) and H and your own knowledge to explain why civilian life had changed for some black American people by 1948.
2. Create two newspaper headlines about the race riots – one from a southern Dixiecrat newspaper and the other from one supporting the NAACP and CORE.
3. What does Source I show you about President Truman's attitude to civil rights?

Practice question

How important was the Second World War in the fight for civil rights? *(For guidance, see pages 113–14.)*

The issue of education

In the 1950s, segregation was still a key feature of life for black American people, and they were subject to what were known as the 'Jim Crow' laws. These were laws passed in the southern states at the end of the nineteenth century to segregate black people from white people in daily life. The Supreme Court had ruled in the *Plessy* v. *Ferguson* case of 1896 that if separate conditions for black people and white people were equal, then segregation was constitutional. This became the separate but equal doctrine – and it was to be challenged in the 1950s, especially in education. Many US states had segregated schools and South Carolina, for example, spent three times more on white-only schools than black-only schools. Figure 3.1 shows the areas where segregation of schools was a matter of state legislation before 1957. Landmark cases, such as *Brown* v. *Board of Education of Topeka*, and the examples of Little Rock High School and James Meredith did remove segregation but there was often unwillingness on the part of many states to embrace the changes.

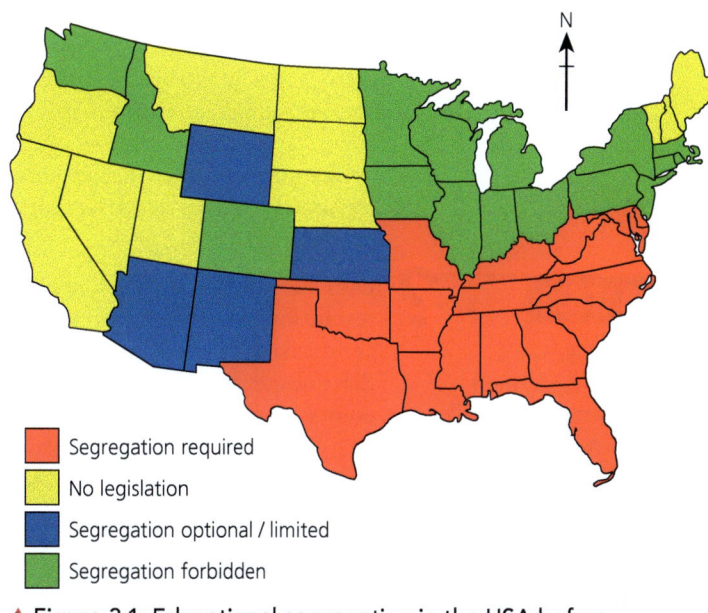

▲ Figure 3.1: Educational segregation in the USA before *Brown* v. *Topeka* case

Brown v. *Topeka*

The first case to challenge segregation in education did not originate in the South, but in Topeka, a town in the mid-west state of Kansas. Linda Brown's parents wanted her to attend a neighbourhood school rather than the school for black American people, which was some distance away. Lawyers from the NAACP, led by Thurgood Marshall, presented evidence to the Supreme Court stating that separate education created low self-esteem and was psychologically harmful. Moreover, the evidence also pointed out that educational achievement was restricted because of this policy. The process took 18 months and the decision was announced on 17 May 1954. Chief Justice Warren of the Supreme Court gave a closing judgment (Source J).

> **Source J:** From the closing judgment of Chief Justice Warren of the Supreme Court at the end of the *Brown* v. *Topeka* case
>
> *Separating white and coloured children in schools has a detrimental effect upon coloured children. The impact is greater when it has the sanction of the law; for the separating of the races is usually interpreted as denoting the inferiority of the Negro group ... We conclude that in the field of public education the doctrine of 'separate but equal' has no place. Separate educational facilities are inherently unequal.*

ACTIVITIES

1. Study Figure 3.1. What does this map show you about segregation in education in the USA before the *Brown* decision?
2. What does Source J show you about the attitude of the Supreme Court towards segregation in education?

Problems after *Brown* v. *Topeka*

However, the *Brown* v. *Topeka* judgment did not specify how integration should be carried out – apart from a vague notion of 'at the earliest possible speed'.

Some areas began to desegregate and, by 1957, more than 300,000 black children were attending schools that had formerly been segregated. However, there were 2.4 million black southern children who were still being educated in Jim Crow schools (separate schools for black American people). Moreover, there were many states, especially in the South, which took deliberate measures to keep separate schools. More than 100 senators and congressmen from the southern states signed the Southern Manifesto, a document that opposed racial integration in education.

Over the next two years, southern state legislatures passed more than 450 laws and resolutions which were aimed to prevent the *Brown* decision being enforced. Despite the decision of the Supreme Court and the open hostility to the *Brown* case, President Eisenhower did little to encourage integration. He was forced into action in 1957 by the events at Little Rock High School.

ACTIVITIES

1. Did the *Brown* v. *Topeka* case bring progress for the civil rights movement? Copy the table below and complete the boxes, explaining your answers.

Yes, because …	No, because …

2. Study Source K. What was the purpose of publishing this photograph?

Practice question

The fight for civil rights during the 1950s was influenced by developments such as:

- The experience of black American people during the Second World War
- The work of the NAACP
- The *Brown* v. *Topeka* case.

Arrange these developments in order of their significance in influencing the campaign for civil rights. *(For guidance, see pages 110–11.)*

▲ **Source K:** Three NAACP lawyers, George Hayes, Thurgood Marshall and James Norbit Jr, celebrating after the *Brown* verdict

Events at Little Rock High School, 1957

After the *Brown* v. *Topeka* decision, Little Rock High School, Arkansas, decided to allow nine black students to enrol. On 3 September 1957, the nine students, led by Elizabeth Eckford, tried to enter the school but were prevented by the state governor, Orval Faubus, who ordered national guardsmen to block their entry. Faubus said there would be public disorder if black students tried to enrol. The following day, 4 September, the National Guard was removed by order of Faubus and the nine students ran the gauntlet of a vicious white crowd. At midday, the students went home under police guard because their safety could not be guaranteed. Press and television coverage in the USA and across the world was a serious embarrassment to a country which put itself forward as the champion of freedom and equality.

President Eisenhower had to act. He sent the 101st Airborne Division consisting of over 1,000 federal troops to Little Rock to protect the black students for the rest of the school year. The 101st patrolled outside the school and escorted the black students into the school. In addition, each of the nine was assigned a personal guard from the 101st who followed them around the school to protect them from the white students. Despite the president's intervention, Faubus closed all Arkansas schools the following year, simply to prevent integration. Many white and most black students had no schooling for a year. Schools in Arkansas re-opened in 1959 following a Supreme Court ruling that schools must integrate.

> **ACTIVITY**
>
> Study Source L. What does it show you about attitudes to integration in the USA in 1957?

◀ **Source L:** Elizabeth Eckford again attempting to enter Little Rock High School, 4 September 1957

The significance of Little Rock

The events at Little Rock were significant for a number of reasons. These are outlined in Figure 3.2.

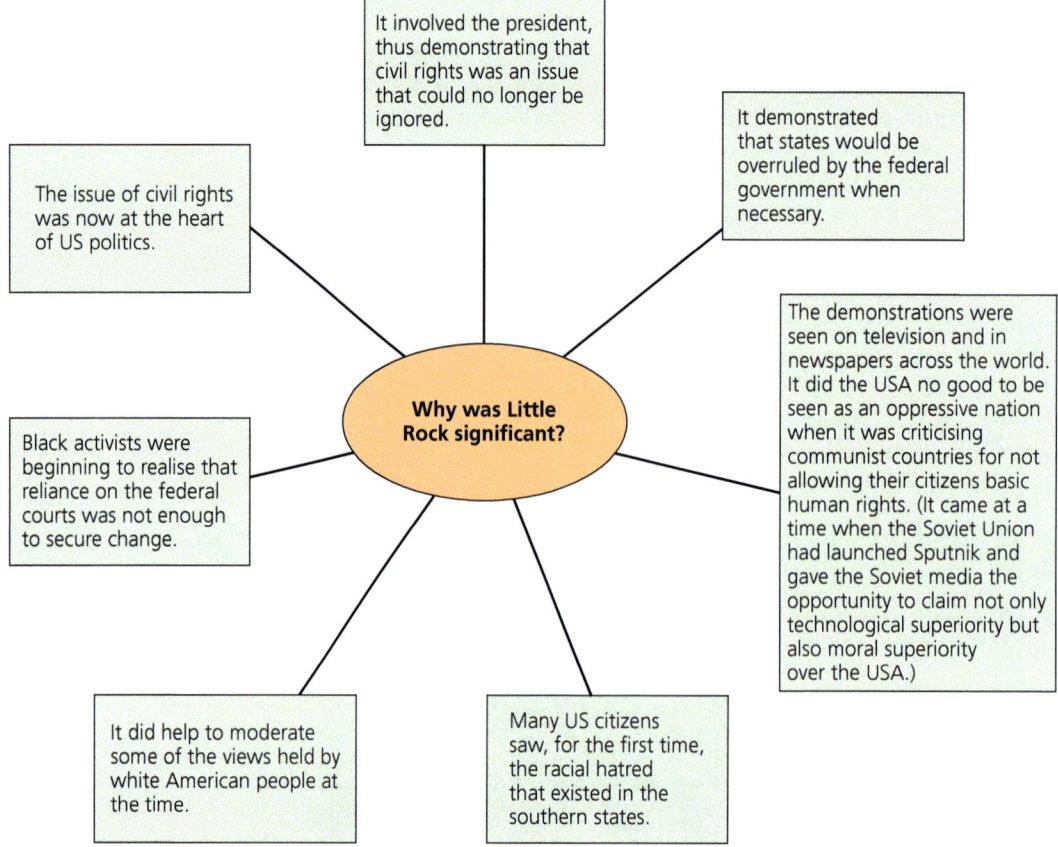

▲ Figure 3.2: The significance of Little Rock

The James Meredith case

In June 1962, the Supreme Court upheld a federal court decision to force Mississippi University to accept the black student James Meredith. The university did not want any black students and Meredith was prevented from registering. In his first major involvement in civil rights, President Kennedy sent in 320 federal marshals to escort Meredith to the campus. There were riots: two people were killed and 166 marshals and 210 demonstrators were wounded. President Kennedy then sent more than 2,000 troops to restore order. The black activists called the event 'The Battle of Oxford'. Three hundred soldiers had to remain on the campus until Meredith received his degree – three years later.

There were some other instances of resistance to integration in education, such as that led by Governor Wallace in Alabama when he tried to stop black American people from enrolling at the state university. Wallace said, 'I am the embodiment of the sovereignty of this state, and I will be present to bar the entrance of any Negro who attempts to enrol at the university.' However, the fact that there had been federal intervention at Mississippi University showed that the tide had turned.

ACTIVITIES

1. Why do you think that education played such an important part in the struggle for civil rights in the 1950s?
2. Did events at Little Rock High School bring progress for the civil rights movement? Copy the table below and complete the boxes to explain your answers.

Yes, because ...	No, because ...

Practice questions

1. How important was education in the struggle for civil rights in the 1950s? *(For guidance, see pages 113–14.)*
2. Explain why the James Meredith case was important for the civil rights movement. *(For guidance, see page 112.)*

The Montgomery bus boycott

Segregation on public transport in the USA had long been a problem for black American people. There had been attempts to end this and there had been some success in the early 1950s in Baton Rouge, Louisiana. The issue came to a head in Montgomery, Alabama, after the arrest of Rosa Parks in December 1955. The rules about segregation on public transport in Montgomery were particularly harsh (Source N).

On 1 December 1955, Rosa Parks boarded a bus in the city of Montgomery and sat with three other black people in the fifth row – the first row that black people could occupy. A few stops later, the first four rows were filled with white people and one white man was left standing. According to the law black and white people could not share the same row, so the bus driver asked all four of the black people seated in the fifth row to move. Three of them moved; Rosa Parks refused.

Rosa Parks was subsequently arrested and from this point the situation escalated into a crisis. Initially, the Montgomery Women's Political Council, led by Jo Ann Robinson, decided to hold a one-day boycott of the buses on Monday 5 December, the day of Parks' trial. On the day after Parks' arrest, Robinson and some students printed thousands of leaflets encouraging people to boycott the city's buses (see Source M).

PUBLIC NOTICE
RULES

- Black American people must follow the instructions of the white drivers.
- The front part of the bus is reserved for white people at all times.
- Black American people must fill the bus from the back.
- Black American people must not sit next to white people and must stand even if there is a vacant seat.
- If a white person boards the bus and all white seats are taken, black people must give up their seats.

▲ Figure 3.3: Montgomery's rules on segregation on public transport

Source M: Part of the leaflet used to encourage the bus boycott, December 1955

Another Negro woman has been arrested and thrown in jail because she refused to get up out of her seat on the bus for a white person to sit down. This has to be stopped. Negroes have rights, too. This woman's case will come up on Monday. We are asking every Negro to stay off the buses Monday in protest of the arrest and trial. If you work, take a cab, or walk. But please, children and grown-ups, don't ride the bus …

ACTIVITY

What does Sources M and N show you about the Montgomery bus boycott?

▲ Source N: Rosa Parks being fingerprinted in Montgomery, 1956

The setting up of the Montgomery Improvement Association

Local civil rights activists, such as Ralph Abernathy and Martin Luther King Jr (the new minister at Dexter Avenue Baptist Church), became involved (Source O). They held a meeting to plan a rally for the evening of the trial and the local NAACP began to prepare its legal challenge to the segregation laws. At the meeting, the Montgomery Improvement Association (MIA) was established to oversee the continuation and maintenance of the boycott and also to improve race relations. King was chosen to lead the MIA because he was quite new to Montgomery and the authorities knew little about him. It is thought that about 20,000 people were involved in the Monday boycott. During the evening of 5 December, some 7,000 attended the planned rally and heard Martin Luther King make an inspirational speech. He explained that African-American people were extremely tired of being humiliated and oppressed in their own country. He said that the patience of African-American people may have seemed as if they did not mind the way they were treated, but now their patience was at an end. However, King was quick to point out that African-American people would not resort to violence, saying 'There will be no cross burnings … we will be guided by law and order.' He emphasised that they would aim to persuade people to follow their cause, rather than use violence.

Rosa Parks was fined US$10 for the offence on the bus and US$4 costs. The MIA decided to continue the boycott until its demands were met. The Montgomery authorities then made a huge error of judgement in refusing the moderates' demands. They pushed King and the MIA to demand complete desegregation on buses.

▼ **Source O:** Martin Luther King addressing leaders of the boycott. Rosa Parks is seated in the front row and on her right is Ralph Abernathy, a leading figure in the black community

ACTIVITIES

1. Why was King keen to put the emphasis on persuasion in his speech of 5 December 1955?
2. What did King mean when he said 'There will be no cross burnings'?
3. Devise some slogans to encourage black American people living in Montgomery in 1955 not to use the public buses.

What happened during the bus boycott?

During the boycott many Montgomery citizens walked to work (Source P), causing the bus company to lose money. Those boycotting the buses were helped during the first few days by black taxi companies. As the boycott progressed, churches bought cars in order to take people to and from work. This created problems because there had to be specific pick-up places for the workers and when people were waiting they were harassed by the police, who used local laws to try to prevent crowds gathering. Many drivers were arrested for minor traffic violations.

Despite their action, the boycotters faced continued intimidation. The Montgomery White Citizens Council led the organised opposition. Membership of this body swelled to almost 12,000 by March 1956, and its membership included some of Montgomery's leading city officials. In some cases the violence used against the boycotters was extreme. King and other leaders had their homes firebombed during 1956. The next step in intimidation came in February 1956, when about 90 of the leading figures, including King and Rosa Parks, were arrested for organising an illegal boycott. King was sentenced to 386 days in jail, instead he paid a fine of US$1,000 in 1957.

As the boycott moved into the summer of 1956, the US national press covered events more closely and this helped raise awareness of the issue of deep racial hatred in the South.

The MIA took the issue of segregation on transport to a federal district court on the basis that it was unconstitutional, citing the *Brown* v. *Topeka* case (see page 31). The federal court accepted that segregation was unconstitutional. However, the Montgomery city officials appealed and the case went to the Supreme Court. On 13 November 1956, the Supreme Court upheld the federal court's decision. The boycott had been successful. It formally came to an end on 20 December 1956 when King, Abernathy and other leaders travelled on an integrated bus.

What was the importance of the bus boycott?

The bus boycott was important because:

- it showed that unity and solidarity (togetherness) could win
- victory offered hope to those who were fighting for improved civil rights
- the NAACP was vindicated in making a legal case and using the *Brown* case (see page 31) as a precedent
- it highlighted the benefits of a peaceful approach and, above all, showed that black American people were able to organise themselves
- it brought King's philosophy to the fore and gave the movement a clear moral framework
- success encouraged King to consider further action that would confront inequality and bring about further change
- it showed the economic power of the black community when the bus company experienced financial problems.

ACTIVITIES

1. What does Source P show you about the Montgomery bus boycott?
2. Write a newspaper article in support of the boycott.

Practice questions

1. Describe the events of the Montgomery bus boycott of 1955–56. *(For guidance, see page 108.)*
2. How important was the Montgomery bus boycott in the struggle for civil rights in the USA? *(For guidance, see pages 113–14.)*

◀ Source P: Montgomery citizens walking to work during the boycott

ACTIVITIES

1. What does Source Q show you about the sit-in protests?
2. Why were the events at Greensboro so important for the civil rights movement?
3. Prepare a one-minute talk to explain why you support the method of the sit-in.

Sit-ins and the fight for equality

The profile of the civil rights movement had been raised by events such as Montgomery and Little Rock and was raised even further by a series of sit-in protests that started in Greensboro, North Carolina in early 1960.

On 1 February 1960 four black students from a local college walked into a F.W. Woolworth store in Greensboro and demanded to be served at a 'whites-only' lunch counter. On being refused they remained seated at the counter until the shop closed (Source Q). The next day, they were accompanied by 27 more students and the day after a further 80 joined them. By the fifth day there were 300 students. The shop agreed to make a few concessions but the students later resumed their protests – some were now arrested for trespass. The students then boycotted any shop in Greensboro that had segregated lunch counters. Sales immediately dropped and eventually segregation ended.

During the sit-ins the students had to endure violence and assaults, but they were careful not to retaliate, copying the peaceful tactics Martin Luther King had used at Montgomery. For the second time, a non-violent approach that hit the local economy through boycotts had been used successfully.

Sit-ins very quickly became a tool of protest, especially in cities where there were many students and in places where black American people had made some progress in civil rights. By August 1961 the sit-ins had attracted over 70,000 participants and resulted in over 3,000 arrests. The technique of the sit-ins was used to allow black people to use other public facilities such as movie theatres. This **direct action** led activists to challenge the deep-rooted racism of the South even further in what became known as the 'freedom rides'.

▼ Source Q: Greensboro students at the Woolworths counter, 2 February 1960

The freedom riders

In December 1960 the Supreme Court decided that all bus stations and terminals that served interstate travellers should be integrated. CORE wanted to test that decision by employing the tactic of the freedom ride. If there was continued failure to carry out the law, CORE would be able to show that narrow-mindedness and racism still existed in the southern states.

The first of the freedom rides began in May 1961 when James Farmer, the National Director of CORE, and 12 volunteers left Washington DC by bus to travel to New Orleans. The black American people used 'whites-only' facilities to ensure integration was taking place. There was little trouble on the first part of the journey. However, at Anniston, Alabama, a bus was attacked and burnt. In Montgomery, white racists beat up several of the freedom riders. In Jackson, Mississippi, 27 freedom riders from the Student Non-violent Coordinating Committee (SNCC) and Southern Christian Leadership Conference (SCLC) were jailed for 67 days for sitting in the 'whites-only' section of the bus station.

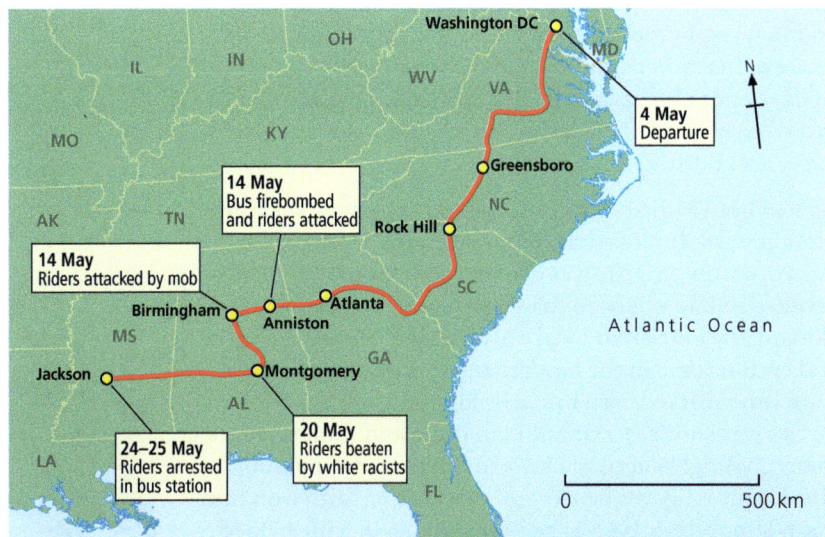

▲ Figure 3.4: Map of the freedom rides, 1961

When the freedom riders reached Birmingham, Alabama, there was no protection for them and they were attacked by an angry mob – the police chief ('Bull' Connor) had given most of the police the day off. Events at Jackson forced the new president, John F. Kennedy, to intervene. Kennedy secured a promise from the state senator that there would be no mob violence. However, when the riders arrived in Jackson, they were immediately arrested when they tried to use the 'whites-only' waiting room.

The freedom riders continued throughout the summer and more than 300 of them were imprisoned in Jackson alone. Attacks on them by the Ku Klux Klan increased. The Attorney General, Robert Kennedy, did not wish to see the situation escalate and was hoping that he would not have to send in US marshals to enforce the law. Violence was avoided in Mississippi when it became clear that marshals would be used. On 22 September the Interstate Commerce Commission issued a regulation that ended racial segregation in bus terminals.

ACTIVITIES

1. Prepare a statement for a local television station to explain why the freedom riders will pass through that area.
2. Why were the freedom rides significant?
3. How successful were the sit-in protesters and the freedom riders?

Practice question

The campaign for civil rights in the 1950s and 1960s was influenced by events such as:
- the Montgomery bus boycott
- the sit-in protests
- the freedom rides.

Arrange these events in order of their significance in helping the campaign to achieve civil rights. *(For guidance, see pages 110–11.)*

The role of Martin Luther King

King was the son of a Baptist minister and grew up in a middle-class home in Atlanta, Georgia. As a teenager he spoke in his father's church and demonstrated that he had a gift for popular speaking. He experienced racial prejudice as a student in such places as Philadelphia, parts of New Jersey and Boston.

He had been minister at the Dexter Avenue Baptist Church, Montgomery, for less than a year when the Montgomery bus boycott began. He was chosen as leader of the MIA because he had not been there long enough to become too close to any particular local organisation. He was energetic and enthusiastic in the boycott and was able to inspire those who worked with him. His idea of using non-violent tactics was similar to Gandhi's in India and soon there were many civil rights activists keen to follow and copy King. His devout religious beliefs and unwavering faith won him many supporters. He was never intimidated. King helped to found the Southern Christian Leadership Conference (SCLC) after the bus boycott. The SCLC was led and run by black people. King and many members of the SCLC felt that boycotts and other forms of non-violent protest should be adopted in the struggle for equality. The SCLC tried to increase the number of black voters with the 'Crusade for Citizenship'. This failed as it did not win support from other civil rights groups and its target of enfranchising 2 million black American people was over-ambitious. Nevertheless, King had become the leading figure in the civil rights movement by 1963.

▲ Martin Luther King

Martin Luther King, 1929–68

1929 Born 15 January

1951 Graduated from Crozer Theological College with a degree in theology

1953 Married Coretta Scott

1955 Led Montgomery bus boycott

1957 Formed and led Southern Christian Leadership Conference

1963 'I have a dream' speech. Voted 'Man of the Year' by *Time* magazine

1964 Winner of the Nobel Peace Prize

1968 4 April, assassinated in Memphis

Source R: From the Nobel Peace Prize citation for Martin Luther King, 1964

He is the first person in the Western world to have shown us that a struggle can be waged without violence. He makes the message of brotherly love a reality in the course of his struggle, and he has brought this message to all nations and races. He has never abandoned his faith in the struggle he is waging, he has been imprisoned on many occasions, his family has been threatened, but he has never faltered.

Practice question

Describe Martin Luther King's career up to the early 1960s. *(For guidance, see page 108.)*

ACTIVITIES

1. What does Source R tell you about Martin Luther King?
2. Why was it significant that the SCLC was led and run by black people?

Martin Luther King and the Birmingham March, 1963

The civil rights issue exploded in 1963. There was still no federal law that made southern states integrate public facilities. In order to avoid desegregating its parks, playgrounds and swimming pools, the city of Birmingham, Alabama, simply closed them all. King and the SCLC sought to challenge the city by using sit-ins and marches to press for desegregation. It was hoped that this would achieve maximum publicity across the USA. Birmingham had a population of about 350,000, of which about 150,000 were black American people. King hoped to mobilise a large part of them in the planned demonstrations.

Demonstrations began in April 1963 after some activists were arrested. Police Chief Eugene 'Bull' Connor then closed all public parks and playgrounds. This prompted King to address a large rally at which he said it was better to go to jail in dignity rather than just accept segregation. King was then arrested in a further demonstration and jailed for defying a ban on marches. During his short stay in prison, he wrote his 'Letter from Birmingham Jail'. This letter became one of the most famous documents of the civil rights movement, and many see it as one of the most powerful in history. Once again, King explained why African-American people were tired and angry at their humiliating treatment in their own country. He pointed out how the citizens of the new independent countries in Africa and Asia had more rights than African-American people and that progress was excruciatingly slow in the USA.

In the letter, King also wrote how he understood that people were impatient for change. He stressed that many in the USA had no idea of the fears that African-American people had and that these fears were felt by all – young and old, male and female. He was keen to point out how the police did little or nothing to stop the hatred and violence and in fact often committed violence themselves against African-American people. Most importantly, King highlighted that there was tremendous poverty among African-American people in a country of incredible wealth.

The situation worsened on King's release from jail when it was decided to use children and students in the demonstrations to test the police reaction. On 3 May, Connor allowed his men to set dogs on the protesters and he then called in the fire department to use powerful water hoses. Connor arrested 2,000 demonstrators as well as almost 1,300 children. Television witnessed the events, which were seen not only across the USA but also all over the world. Photographs of the demonstration and police reaction were published in national newspapers. This gave King all the publicity he wanted. It showed the violence of the authorities in the face of peaceful demonstrators. By early May there was chaos in Birmingham.

At this stage President Kennedy became involved. He sent the Assistant Attorney General, Burke Marshall, to mediate between the parties. Talks between King and the Birmingham city leaders resulted in a settlement on 9 May and it was agreed that desegregation in the city would take place within 90 days.

A consequence of the violence was Kennedy's decision to bring in a Civil Rights Bill. On the same day, Medgar Evers, leader of the Mississippi NAACP, was shot dead in Jackson by a white sniper.

▲ **Source S:** Police dogs attacking civil rights demonstrators in Birmingham, Alabama, 3 May 1963

ACTIVITIES

1 Work in pairs. Find King's 'Letter from Birmingham Jail' on the Martin Luther King Centre website. Prepare a presentation for the class and choose what you consider to be the ten most important points of the letter.

2 What does Source S show you about police methods in Birmingham?

Practice question

Explain why events in Birmingham were important in the campaign for civil rights. *(For guidance, see page 112.)*

Martin Luther King and the march on Washington, 1963

After Birmingham, the civil rights groups wanted to maintain their high profile and the idea of a march on Washington DC was put forward by A. Philip Randolph (see page 28). The NAACP, CORE, SNCC and SCLC all took part in organising the march. King was keen to march because he knew that there were those within the civil rights movement who felt that progress was slow and he worried that these people might drift towards violence if the high profile was not sustained. The Washington police put a hold on leave for its 3,000 officers in case there was violence. President Kennedy, fearing violence, asked the organisers to call off the march.

The march began as a call for jobs and freedom, but it broadened to cover the aims of the whole of the civil rights movement. There was naturally a demand for the passage of Kennedy's Civil Rights Bill.

The march

When the march took place, on 28 August 1963, there were about 250,000 demonstrators. The organisers had expected less than half this figure. People came from all over the USA. When politicians were seen, there were chants of 'pass the bill' (referring to Kennedy's Civil Rights Bill). King was the final speaker of the day and his speech has now become part of the lore of the struggle for civil rights. He used his skills as an orator and included many biblical references, which appealed to all sections in society. In the speech he quoted from the American Declaration of Independence and looked to a future where he saw racial equality in the USA.

▲ Source T: Martin Luther King at the Lincoln Memorial, 28 August 1963

3 The issue of civil rights, 1941–70

The march on Washington was hailed as a great success. It was televised across the USA and did much for the civil rights movement. It brought together different sections of US society and put further pressure on President Kennedy to move forward on civil rights.

After the march, King and the other leaders met President Kennedy to discuss civil rights legislation. Kennedy was keen to let them know of his own commitment to the Civil Rights Bill. However, all at the meeting were aware there were many Republican politicians still opposed to any change.

King's hopes began to seem illusory. In September 1963 four black girls were killed in a bomb attack while attending Sunday school in Birmingham. The civil rights movement seemed to stall in late 1963 and was then hit by the assassination of President Kennedy.

The new President, Lyndon Johnson, pushed Kennedy's Civil Rights Bill through Congress and it became law in 1964. However, it did not guarantee black American people the vote, so, in 1965, King decided to hold another non-violent campaign at Selma, Alabama. He decided to hold a march from Selma to Birmingham, to present a petition demanding voting rights. The marchers were attacked by police and state troopers. This became known as 'Bloody Sunday'. In response to this, on 15 March, President Johnson, in a speech to Congress, called for passage of a Voting Rights Act that would enfranchise black American people. The Act was passed in August 1965: King's policy of non-violence had worked. After 1965, King broadened his work and moved to the North to help the poor black American people. He also became prominent in the anti-Vietnam War movement and the 'Poor People's Campaign'.

Martin Luther King's assassination

On 3 April 1968 (the day before his assassination), King gave a speech at a church rally in which he spoke of his hopes and fears for the future. In the speech he spoke of 'having been to the mountain top' and said '... we as people will get to the Promised Land!' Prophetically, King said he was not concerned about living a long life.

The following day, on 4 April 1968, Martin Luther King visited Memphis to support black refuse collectors who were striking for equal treatment with their white co-workers. The economic and educational gulf between black and white people was still great, not only in the South but also in the North. King was shot on that same day in Memphis. James Earl Ray, a white racist, was arrested and jailed for the crime, but there is still doubt over whether he was the real killer.

On his death, there was a final outburst of rioting across the country. Forty-six people died; more than 3,000 were injured in violent clashes and demonstrations across more than 100 cities. This was a great irony – it seemed as if King's whole work and life had been for nothing.

Practice questions
1. Explain why the assassination of Martin Luther King resulted in a wave of rioting across the USA. *(For guidance, see page 112.)*
2. How far did the work of Martin Luther King contribute to the securing of civil rights for black American people? *(For guidance, see page 109.)*

ACTIVITIES
1. Find Martin Luther King's 'I have a dream' speech on the Martin Luther King Centre website. Can you suggest reasons why it has become one of the most famous speeches in history?
2. Find King's 'I have been to the mountain top' speech on the Martin Luther King Centre website. What do you think he meant when he said 'We as a people will get to the Promised Land'?

The role of Malcolm X

Malcolm X and the Nation of Islam

For some in the civil rights movement, progress had been painfully slow and a feeling grew that Martin Luther King's methods would never bring equality in politics and equality of opportunity in life. A group which had never accepted King's ideas was the Nation of Islam (or Black Muslims) – its supporters openly sought separatism. Members rejected their slave surnames and called themselves 'X'.

The most famous member of the Nation of Islam was Malcolm X, and his brilliant oratory skills helped to increase membership to about 100,000 between 1952 and 1964. He was a superb organiser and during the time he was a member of the Nation of Islam, he travelled across the USA winning converts. Malcolm X helped to set up educational and social programmes for black youths in ghettos. By 1960, more than 75 per cent of the membership of the Nation of Islam was aged between 17 and 35. He is credited with re-connecting black American people with their African heritage and is responsible for the spread of Islam in the black community in the USA. His influence on people such as Stokely Carmichael (see page 50) was crucial.

Many members of the mainstream civil rights groups did not like the Nation of Islam and some felt that the Muslims had a 'hate-white doctrine', which was as dangerous as any white racist group. Thurgood Marshall (see pages 31 and 55) said that the Nation of Islam was run by a 'bunch of thugs organised from prisons and financed by some Arab group'. Such criticism never concerned Malcolm X and he was never afraid to attack King and other leaders of the civil rights movement. He criticised the 1963 march on Washington, which he called 'the farce on Washington'. He could not understand why so many black people were impressed by 'a demonstration run by whites in front of a statue of a president who has been dead for a hundred years and who didn't like us when he was alive'.

▲ Malcolm X

> **Source U:** From a speech by Malcolm X in New York, 12 December 1964
>
> *I believe in the brotherhood of man, all men, but I don't believe in brotherhood with anybody who doesn't want brotherhood with me. I believe in treating people right, but I'm not going to waste my time trying to treat somebody right who doesn't know how to return the treatment.*

Malcolm X, 1925–65

- 1925 Born Malcolm Little in Omaha
- 1931 Father was murdered by white supremacists
- 1942 Lived in New York, involved in pimping and drug dealing
- 1946 Found guilty of burglary and imprisoned
- 1952 Released from jail. Had become a follower of the Nation of Islam. Changed his name to 'X'
- 1958 Married Betty Shabazz
- 1964 Left the Nation of Islam and formed Muslim Mosque, Inc. and the black nationalist Organisation of Afro-American Unity
- 1964 Went on pilgrimage to Mecca. His political and religious views altered. Changed his name to Malik El-Hajj Shabazz
- 1965 21 February, shot by three members of the Nation of Islam

The influence of Malcolm X

Malcolm X had a tremendous influence on young urban black American people. He felt that violence could be justified not only for self-defence but also as a means to secure a separate black nation. However, after a visit to Mecca he changed his views and left the Black Muslims to set up the Muslim Mosque, Inc. and the Organisation of Afro-American Unity to promote closer ties between Africans and African-American people. Malcolm X said the trip to Mecca allowed him to see Muslims of different races interacting as equals. He came to believe that Islam could be the means by which racial problems could be overcome. He pushed to end racial discrimination in the USA, but this brought him enemies, particularly among the Black Muslim population. In February 1965 Malcolm X and his family survived the firebombing of their home in the Queen's district of New York. The following week Malcolm X was assassinated by three black Muslims. He was shot several times as he began a speech to 400 of his followers at the Audubon Ballroom just outside the district of Harlem in New York.

Malcolm X's views and ideas became the foundation of the more radical civil rights movements such as Black Power (see pages 50–1) and the Black Panthers (see pages 52–3). Many historians have said that Malcolm X helped raise the self-esteem of black American people more than any other individual in the civil rights movement.

> **Source V:** From Malcolm X's speech at the Founding Rally of the Organisation of Afro-American Unity, 28 June 1964
>
> We have formed an organisation known as the Organisation of Afro-American Unity which has the same aim and objective to fight whoever gets in our way, to bring about the complete independence of people of African descent here in the Western Hemisphere, and first here in the United States, and bring about the freedom of these people by any means necessary. That's our motto. We want freedom by any means necessary. We want justice by any means necessary. We want equality by any means necessary.

> **Source W:** From Malcolm X's funeral oration, given by the black American actor Ossie Davis
>
> Many will ask what Harlem finds to honor in this stormy, controversial and bold young captain – and we will smile. They will say he is of hate – a fanatic, a racist ... and we will answer 'Did you ever talk to Brother Malcolm? Did you ever really listen to him? Did he ever do a mean thing? Was he ever associated with violence or any public disturbance?' ... in honoring him, we honor the best in ourselves.

ACTIVITIES

1. Why did Malcolm choose the name 'X'?
2. What does Source U show you about Malcolm X's attitude to racism?
3. Study Source V. What methods does Malcolm X suggest using to bring about change in the position of black American people?
4. How reliable was Source W about Malcolm X? Explain your answer using the sources and your own knowledge.

Practice questions

1. Describe the work of Malcolm X in the 1950s. *(For guidance, see page 108.)*
2. How important was Malcolm X in the campaign for civil rights? *(For guidance, see page 109.)*
3. The campaign for civil rights during the 1960s was influenced by the leadership of the following individuals:
   - ☐ Martin Luther King
   - ☐ Malcolm X
   - ☐ Bull Connor

   Arrange these individuals in order of their significance in influencing the campaign for civil rights. *(For guidance, see pages 110–11.)*

Civil rights legislation

The Civil Rights Act 1964

Following the assassination of President Kennedy, his successor, Lyndon Johnson, was able to push the Civil Rights Bill through the House of Representatives and the Senate, ensuring that those southern Democrats who opposed the Bill would be counterbalanced by Republicans. Johnson had been in high-level politics since 1938 and he needed all his skills to persuade and cajole the Republicans to vote with him. He had put forward his vision of a 'Great Society' (see pages 56–7) which would attack racial injustice and poverty. This was in the same spirit as Kennedy's 'New Frontier' (see pages 54–5).

There was deep shock within the USA following Kennedy's assassination and there were those in Congress who voted sympathetically for the Bill. Johnson was able to win some support in Congress because he was a southerner, from Texas.

The Civil Rights Act is seen by many as President Johnson's greatest achievement. However, there were many black American people who criticised it as being insufficient and coming rather late in the day. In addition to this, there were many white American people in the South who resented it and strove to make it fail.

The Civil Rights Act 1964

- Segregation in hotels, motels, restaurants, lunch counters and theatres was banned.
- The Act placed the responsibility on the federal government to bring cases to court where discrimination still occurred.
- Any business engaged in transactions with the government was monitored to ensure there was no discrimination.
- Black students were given equal rights to enter all public places and bodies which received government money, including schools.
- The Fair Employment Practices Commission, which had been set up during the Second World War (see page 28), was established on a permanent basis.
- The Act created the Equal Employment Opportunity Commission (EEOC) to implement the law.

Practice questions

1. Explain why some black and some white American people criticised the Civil Rights Act 1964. *(For guidance, see page 112.)*
2. How important was the Civil Rights Act 1964? *(For guidance see pages 113–14.)*

▼ **Source X:** President Johnson signing the Civil Rights Act on 2 July 1964. Martin Luther King is standing behind him

3 The issue of civil rights, 1941–70

Selma and voting rights

In 1870, by the Fifteenth Amendment, male black American people were given the right to vote. However, some states disenfranchised them by such means as unfair taxation and literacy tests. The literacy tests were not a test of reading and writing – they asked difficult arithmetic and cultural questions, which most people would have found impossible.

In 1962, the US government set up the Voter Education Project. The Project was staffed mainly by members of the SNCC and they spent much time with eligible voters showing them how to register and overcome the barriers that were placed in front of them – for example, the mathematical questions that were impossible to answer. The project did result in more than 650,000 new voter registrations, but many people were still refused the right to vote on dubious grounds. The SNCC workers were subject to harassment – in Georgia, several churches were bombed, workers were beaten up and some were shot. Those who did register and subsequently voted were sometimes evicted from their land, sacked from their job and refused credit.

In 1965, Martin Luther King and his colleagues decided to force the issue by embarking on another non-violent campaign. The town of Selma, Alabama, was to be the battleground as there were only 383 black American voters who had been able to register out of a possible 15,000. The sheriff of Selma, Jim Clark, had a reputation to match that of 'Bull' Connor in Birmingham (see pages 39 and 41). King was hoping for a brutal reaction to his demonstrations because he knew that the press and television would again highlight the continued bigotry of the South.

There were 2 months of attempts to register black voters and 2 months of rejections. King and his followers were subjected to beatings and arrests. One demonstrator was murdered. It was decided to hold a march from Selma to the state capital, Birmingham, in order to present Governor Wallace with a petition asking for voting rights. Governor Wallace banned the march but King was determined to take his supporters and lobby Wallace.

The march took place on 7 March but was stopped on the Edmund Pettus Bridge where the marchers were attacked by Sheriff Clark's men and state troopers (see Source Y). The marchers faced tear gas, mounted police and clubs, and were forced to return to Selma. This became known as 'Bloody Sunday' and the event forced President Johnson's hand. A second march took place two days later but King turned the marchers back – he had agreed with Johnson that he would avoid violent confrontation with Clark again.

Public opinion across the USA was firmly behind King and the civil rights movements, and on 15 March President Johnson promised to put forward a bill that would enfranchise black American people. Eventually, it was agreed that a march from Selma to Montgomery would go ahead if it was peaceful. King led more than 25,000 people on 21 March – this was the biggest event that had ever been seen in the South.

> **ACTIVITIES**
>
> 1. What does Source Y show you about the civil rights march from Selma?
> 2. Was King justified in putting the lives of his followers at risk in the Selma marches? Explain your answer.
> 3. How successful were the Selma marches?

▼ Source Y: The civil rights march to the Edmund Pettus Bridge, Selma, 7 March 1965

The Voting Rights Act 1965

The success of the Selma march created an atmosphere of optimism and, in the summer, President Johnson introduced the Voting Rights Bill which was quickly enacted by Congress. The Act:

- ended literacy tests
- ensured federal agents could monitor registration – and step in if it was felt there was discrimination (it was thought that if less than 50 per cent of all its voting-age citizens were registered then racial discrimination could be presumed).

By the end of 1965, 250,000 black American people had registered to vote (one-third had been assisted by government monitors who checked that the law was being followed). A further 750,000 registered by the end of 1968 (see Table 3.1 for further registered voters data). Furthermore, the number of elected black representatives increased rapidly after the Act.

State	White people registered (%)	Black people registered (%)
Alabama	94.6	61.3
Arkansas	81.6	77.9
Florida	94.2	67.0
Georgia	88.5	60.4
Louisiana	87.1	60.8
Mississippi	89.8	66.5
North Carolina	78.4	53.7
South Carolina	71.5	54.6
Tennessee	92.0	92.1
Texas	61.8	73.1
Virginia	78.7	58.9
USA as a whole	80.4	64.8

▲ Table 3.1: Registered voters in certain states in the USA, 1969

King's policy of non-violence appeared to have worked. There was widespread support and sympathy from white American people, and there had been two key pieces of legislation which had removed discrimination and disenfranchisement.

However, other groups were emerging that opposed King's idea of non-violence. There was a feeling among some that progress was slow and that, too often, King had been ready to make deals with the white authorities (see pages 41–7).

Further civil rights reforms were introduced before President Johnson left office in 1968:

- 1967: the Supreme Court declared that state laws forbidding interracial marriages were unconstitutional
- 1968: Fair Housing Act – discrimination in housing based on race, colour, gender, national origin, or religion was outlawed.

ACTIVITIES

1. What can you learn from Table 3.1 about voters in the USA in 1969?
2. Re-read the sections on the Civil Rights Act (page 46) and the Voting Rights Act (above). Which do you think was the more important? Copy and complete the table below.

Civil Rights Act more important because …	Voting Rights Act more important because …

Practice questions

1. How important was the Selma campaign in the fight to secure equal voting rights for black American people? *(For guidance see pages 113–14.)*
2. How far had Martin Luther King's dream of equal treatment for black American people come true by the end of 1968? *(For guidance see page 109.)*

Race riots in the 1960s

Despite the civil rights laws, many young black American people were frustrated, and those living in the ghettos felt anger at the high rates of unemployment, continuing discrimination and poverty. On 11 August 1965, this frustration exploded into a major riot involving 30,000 people in the Watts district of Los Angeles. The riot left 34 dead, 1,072 injured, 4,000 arrested and caused about US$40 million of damage. There were riots across the USA's major cities in the two following summers. Many of the riots followed a similar pattern – the arrest of a black youth, a police raid, rumours of police brutality and then the explosion of the riot.

Racial violence peaked in the summer of 1967, when there were riots in 125 US cities. The two largest riots occurred in July: Newark left 26 dead and over 1,000 injured, and Detroit left more than 40 people dead, hundreds injured and 7,000 arrested. During the three summers of riots, more than 130 people were killed and damage totalled more than US$700 million.

The riots of 1965–67 caused President Johnson and his advisers to look into the factors behind them. The Kerner Report (1968) stated that racism was deeply embedded in American society. It not only highlighted the economic issues faced by black American people but also the 'systematic police bias and brutality' and recommended federal initiatives which would mean increased expenditure. The report was largely ignored.

The year of 1968 did seem to be the end of an era. The Vietnam War had begun to dominate the domestic scene and the student movement also took centre stage. However, there had been significant changes and the civil rights legislation of the 1960s had given equality and protection before the law. Yet the riots of 1965–67 and those that erupted on the death of Martin Luther King in 1968 indicated that there was still huge frustration among the black population.

> **ACTIVITIES**
> 1. What does Source Z show you about the riot in Detroit?
> 2. What was the significance of the Kerner Report?
> 3. Why has 1968 been seen as the 'end of an era'?

▼ **Source Z:** The National Guard and police facing rioters in Detroit, 1967

The Black Power movement

Despite the progress of the late 1950s and early 1960s, many young black American people were frustrated. Out of this frustration the Black Power movement emerged. Black Power was originally a political slogan but it came to cover a wide range of activities in the late 1960s which aimed to increase the power of black people in American life. Stokely Carmichael and others in the SNCC (see page 39) wanted black people to take responsibility for their own lives and to reject white help. For some black activists, Black Power meant separation, but for others it was a way of ridding the USA of a corrupt power structure. Carmichael and his associates wanted black American people to create their own political force so they would not have to rely on the black groupings that existed at the time, such as the NAACP, CORE and the SCLC. Carmichael and his followers wanted black people to have pride in their heritage and they adopted the slogan 'Black is beautiful'. They wanted black American people to develop a feeling of black pride and promoted African forms of dress and appearance.

Carmichael attracted criticism because of his aggressive attitude and was attacked when he denounced the involvement of the USA in the Vietnam War. He eventually left the SNCC and became associated with the Black Panthers, but left the USA and moved to Guinea in 1969 where he lived until his death in 1998.

▲ Stokely Carmichael

Stokely Carmichael, 1941–98

1941	Born in Port of Spain, Trinidad and Tobago
1943	Moved to New York City
1960	Attended Howard University, Washington DC (gained a degree in philosophy)
1961	Took part in the freedom rides; jailed for seven weeks
1966	Chairman of the SNCC
1966	27th arrest; made his 'Black Power' speech
1967	Wrote *Black Power*
1968	Joined the Black Panthers
1969	Left the USA and moved to Guinea. Changed his name to Kwame Ture
1998	Died in Guinea

Source AA: From a speech made in 1966 by Stokely Carmichael, leader of the SNCC, describing his own frustrations and those of many black American people. He had just been released from police custody following involvement in a civil rights march in Mississippi

This is the twenty-seventh time I have been arrested. I ain't going to jail no more. The only way we gonna stop them white men from whuppin' us is to take over. We been saying freedom for six years and we ain't got nothin'. What we gonna start sayin' now is Black Power!

3 The issue of civil rights, 1941–70

The Mexico Olympics, 1968

The Black Power movement gained tremendous publicity at the 1968 Mexico City Olympics, at the winners' ceremonies for the Men's 200 metres and 400 metres relay (Source BB). The athletes wore part of the movement's uniform – a single black glove and black beret – and also gave the clenched fist salute. During the ceremony, when the US national anthem was being played, Tommie Smith gave the salute with his right hand to indicate Black Power and John Carlos with his left to show black unity. Smith also wore a black scarf to represent black pride and black socks with no shoes to represent black poverty in racist America. Smith and Carlos were sent back to the USA. They were accused of bringing politics into sport and damaging the Olympic spirit. On their return, they both received several death threats.

Peter Norman, the Australian who came second in the 200 metres, also showed his support for the Black Power cause by wearing an OPHR (Olympic Project for Human Rights) badge. The Australian Olympic Committee was furious at his actions and did not select him for the 1972 Olympics. Norman died on 3 October 2006 and both Tommie Smith and John Carlos gave eulogies and were pallbearers at his funeral.

As a result of these athletes' actions, the whole world was now aware of the Black Power movement.

> **Source CC:** From a press conference given by Tommie Smith in October 1968, following the Olympic medal ceremony
>
> *If I win, I am American, not a black American. But if I did something bad, then they would say I am a Negro. We are black and we are proud of being black. Black America will understand what we did tonight.*

▲ **Source BB:** Tommie Smith and John Carlos at the 1968 Olympic Games in Mexico City. Smith won the gold medal and Carlos the bronze in the 200 metres. The silver medallist, Peter Norman (left), wears a badge to show his support for the American athletes

ACTIVITIES

1. What does Source AA tell you about Stokely Carmichael?
2. What can you learn from Sources EE and FF (pages 52–3) about Black Power?
3. Working in pairs, prepare a case to support and a case to condemn the actions of US athletes at the Mexico City Olympics in 1968.

Practice questions

1. Describe the Black Power movement. *(For guidance, see page 108.)*
2. How important was Stokely Carmichael in the struggle for civil rights? *(For guidance, see pages 113–14.)*

The Black Panther movement

At the same time as the urban riots (see page 49) and the development of 'Black Power', there emerged the 'Black Panthers'. This party was founded by Huey Newton and Bobby Seale in October 1966 in Oakland, California (see Source DD) . Both men had been heavily influenced by Malcolm X. The Panthers had a 10-point programme and were prepared to use revolutionary means to achieve these aims (see Source EE).

The Black Panthers were even prepared to form alliances with radical white groups if it was felt it would help bring down the 'establishment'. The leaders of the Panthers advocated an end to capitalism and the establishment of a socialist society. Seale constantly stated: 'We believe our fight is a class struggle and not a race struggle.'

The Panthers wore uniforms and were prepared to use weapons, training members in their use. By the end of 1968, they had 5,000 members. However, internal divisions and the events of 1969, which saw 27 Panthers killed and 700 injured in confrontations with the police, saw support diminish. They were constantly targeted by the FBI and by 1982 the party had disbanded.

> **Source EE:** The Black Panthers' 10-point programme, October 1966
> 1. Freedom. We want power to determine the destiny of our Black Community.
> 2. We want full employment for our people.
> 3. We want an end to the robbery by the white man of our Black Community.
> 4. We want decent housing, fit for shelter of human beings.
> 5. We want education for our people that exposes the true nature of this decadent American society. We want education that teaches us our true history and our role in the present-day society.
> 6. We want all black men to be exempt from military service.
> 7. We want an immediate end to police brutality and murder of black people.
> 8. We want freedom for all black men held in federal, state, county and city prisons and jails.
> 9. We want all black people when brought to trial to be tried in court by a jury of their peer group or people from their black communities, as defined by the Constitution of the United States.
> 10. We want land, bread, housing, education, clothing, justice and peace.

▲ **Source DD:** Bobby Seale, left, and Huey Newton, co-founders of the Black Panther Party for Self Defence

Achievements of the Black Panthers

Despite constant harassment from the FBI and police (Source FF), the Black Panthers were able to point to some successes during their existence. They established the 'Free Breakfast for Children Program' in parts of California and Chicago. In addition, they provided clothing distribution centres, gave guidance on drugs rehabilitation and assistance to those who had relatives in prison.

▲ **Source GG:** The symbol of the Black Panther Party

> **Source FF:** J. Edgar Hoover, FBI Director, on 15 June 1969, reproduced in Reginald Major, *A Panther is a Black Cat*, published 2007
>
> *The Black Panthers are the greatest threat to the internal security of the country. Schooled in communist ideology and the teaching of Chinese Communist leader Mao Tse-tung, its members have perpetrated numerous assaults on police officers and have engaged in violent confrontations with police throughout the country. Leaders and representatives of the Black Panther Party travel extensively all over the United States preaching their gospel of hate and violence not only to ghetto residents, but to students in colleges, universities and high schools as well.*

Practice question

The campaign for securing equality for black American people during the 1960s was influenced by developments such as:

- the Black Power movement
- the leadership of Malcolm X
- the Black Panther movement.

Arrange these developments in order of their significance in influencing the campaign for securing equality for black American people. *(For guidance, see pages 110–11.)*

ACTIVITIES

1. What image does Source DD project of the Black Panthers?
2. Study Source EE. Which of these aims do you think Martin Luther King would have opposed and why?
3. Study Source FF. Explain why the Black Panther movement was seen as a threat to US society.
4. How successful was the Black Panther movement?
5. What were the most important factors in bringing about improved civil rights for black American people between 1950 and 1963?

    In your answer you may wish to discuss the following:
    - ☐ the campaign for equality in education
    - ☐ the campaign for equality in public transport
    - ☐ the role of Martin Luther King
    - ☐ the role of Malcolm X
    - ☐ and any other relevant factors.
6. Working in pairs, copy the table below and complete it using the information from this chapter.

What had been achieved for black American people by 1965?	What were the remaining issues for black American people after 1965?

4 Political change, 1960–2000

There was much political change within the USA during the years 1960–2000. The period began with the tremendous optimism generated by the young President Kennedy, which then faltered following his assassination. President Johnson was able to bring about civil rights reforms and social reforms with his Great Society programme but the USA was torn apart by its involvement in the Vietnam War and the Watergate Scandal. Presidents Reagan and Clinton tried to return stability to the USA but each experienced problems ranging from economic issues to personal scandals.

The domestic policies of Kennedy

In the 1960s Presidents Kennedy and Johnson introduced a series of important changes to US society known as the New Frontier and the Great Society.

Kennedy and the New Frontier

Kennedy won the presidential election campaign of 1960 and was president until his assassination in 1963. In his acceptance speech as president he mentioned the 'New Frontier'.

At first it was simply a slogan to try to unite and inspire the American people and get them behind him. However, it soon became a programme of reform and change through which Kennedy hoped to make the USA a fairer society by giving equal rights to all black people, and by helping them to better themselves. He called it the New Frontier to make people feel excited and try to reduce opposition to it. Above all else he wanted to make the USA a fairer and better place and he asked American people to join him in being 'New Frontiersmen'.

Opposition to the New Frontier

Kennedy faced opposition in Congress to his ideas.

- His own position as president was not strong as he had won only by a narrow margin in the 1960 presidential campaign.
- Many older members of Congress felt he was too young and inexperienced and distrusted his Brains Trust appointments.
- Some were suspicious of the radical nature of his 'New Frontier' and the pace of change and saw it as a socialist programme.
- He was the first Catholic president (see Source A). This again created suspicion from the more traditional Protestant politicians.
- The greatest opposition came from Southern Congressmen, even Democrats – members of his own party – who disliked his commitment to civil rights. They felt that equal rights for black American people would cost them the votes of white people in the South.

Despite his charm and charisma, Kennedy found it difficult to deal with Congress and many of his bills were rejected. However, he was successful in increasing social security, raising the minimum wage and setting up training schemes for the unemployed. His early death meant he was unable to complete his programme of reform.

	The New Frontier
Civil rights	1 Kennedy appointed five federal judges, including Thurgood Marshall. Marshall was a black American and was a leading civil rights activist. 2 Kennedy threatened legal action against the state of Louisiana for refusing to fund schools which were not segregated. 3 In October 1962, Kennedy sent 23,000 government troops to ensure that one black student, James Meredith, could study at the University of Mississippi (page 34). 4 Kennedy introduced a Civil Rights Bill to Congress in February 1963. This aimed to give black people equality in housing and education but was defeated in Congress.
The economy	1 Kennedy deliberately decided not to balance the budget in order to increase economic growth and reduce unemployment. 2 He introduced a general tax cut. More spending would mean more goods sold. 3 There were also public works that cost US$900 million. The federal government began a series of projects, such as new roads and public buildings. 4 Grants were given to high-tech companies to invest in high-tech equipment with which to train workers. 5 There was increased spending on defence and space technology, all of which secured or created jobs. Kennedy also promised that the USA would put a man on the moon by the end of the 1960s.
Social reform	1 Kennedy planned to increase the minimum wage from US$1.00 to US$1.25 an hour. 2 Kennedy planned to start Medicare, a cheap system of state health insurance. 3 The Manpower and Training Act 1962 provided retraining for the long-term unemployed. 4 The Area Redevelopment Act 1961 allowed the federal government to give loans and grants to states with long-term unemployment. 5 The Housing Act 1961 provided cheap loans for the redevelopment of inner cities. 6 The Social Security Act 1962 gave greater financial help to the elderly and unemployed. Social security benefits were extended to each child whose father was unemployed.

▲ Table 4.1: The key measures of the New Frontier

ACTIVITIES

1. Study Source A. Suggest reasons why some people in the USA were concerned that President Kennedy was Roman Catholic.
2. How successful was the New Frontier policy?

Practice questions

1. Describe the aims of Kennedy's New Frontier. *(For guidance, see page 108.)*
2. Explain why there was opposition to the New Frontier. *(For guidance, see page 112.)*

◀ Source A: John F. Kennedy shakes hands with Father Richard J. Casey, the pastor, after attending Mass at Holy Trinity

The domestic policies of Johnson

Lyndon Johnson was president from 1963 to 1968. His achievements have often been underestimated and overlooked due to the reputation of his predecessor, Kennedy, and the US involvement in the war in Vietnam.

Great Society

Johnson decided to continue the work of Kennedy and to take it further. In his first speech as president he talked of a 'Great Society', which would declare war on poverty. To do this he planned to improve the health of the poor and the old by providing them with a better diet and living conditions. He called for 'an immediate end to racial injustice', especially racial discrimination in employment and education. Johnson tackled areas that Kennedy had not been able to improve such as medical care for the poor.

Johnson was an experienced politician who knew how to get things done and how to make deals with Congress. He was far more successful than nearly any other president in getting measures passed through Congress. Also, because he was a Southerner, he knew how to deal with the Southern Democrats and overcome their opposition – especially to civil rights. Some believe his six-foot-three-inch frame helped him to dominate others.

	The Great Society
Civil rights	1. The Civil Rights Act of 1964 banned discrimination in public places, in federally assisted programmes and in employment. 2. The Civil Rights Act set up the Equal Opportunity Commission to implement the law. 3. The Voting Rights Act 1965 appointed agents to ensure that voting procedures were carried out properly (see pages 43 and 45). 4. In 1967, the Supreme Court declared all laws banning interracial marriages were to be removed.
Economy	1. Johnson cut taxes to give consumers more money to spend and, in turn, to help businesses grow and create more jobs. 2. Johnson improved railways and highways. 3. The Appalachian Recovery Programme provided federal funds for the development of the Appalachians, a mountainous area in the eastern states. 4. Manufacturers and shops had to label goods fairly and clearly. Consumers had the right to return faulty goods and exchange them.
Social reform	1. The Medical Care Act 1965 provided Medicare (for older people) and Medicaid for people living in poverty. This was an attempt to try to ensure that all American people had equal access to health care. 2. The Elementary and Secondary Education Act, also of 1965, provided the first major federal support for state education ever. Federal money was provided to try to ensure that standards of education in all states were equal. 3. The Model Cities Act 1966 continued Kennedy's policy of urban renewal. It was in the centres of the big cities that living conditions were at their worst and where crime was highest. The act provided federal funds for slum clearance and the provision of better services. 4. The minimum wage was increased from US$1.25 to US$1.40 an hour. 5. US$1.5 billion was spent on the Head Start Programme so that teachers could provide additional education for very young children from poor backgrounds. 6. The Office of Economic Opportunity set up schemes to help people in inner cities who were living in poverty. It funded new education projects and community projects and provided loans for local schemes. These schemes were the basis of Johnson's Programme for Poverty.

▲ Table 4.2: The key measures of the Great Society

4 Political change, 1960–2000

Opposition to the Great Society

Just like Kennedy with his policies, Johnson faced powerful opposition to his Great Society measures. This opposition, however, was distorted due to attitudes to US involvement in the war in Vietnam.

- Republicans accused him of wasting money on welfare programmes and of undermining 'rugged individualism'. He was accused of overspending on welfare programmes.
- He was accused of doing too little to tackle the problems of the inner cities. In 1967 there was serious rioting in several cities, including six days in Watts, the black district of Los Angeles.
- The greatest problem for Johnson was the escalation of the US involvement in the war in Vietnam. This was not only costly, meaning spending was diverted from the Great Society to paying for the war, but it led to increasing criticism of Johnson himself (see pages 89–93). His great election victory of 1964 seemed in the distant past as many American people celebrated his decision not to run for re-election as president in 1968.

The Train Robbery

▲ **Source C:** A cartoon showing President Johnson and the Great Society, from the British magazine *Punch*, 1967. It shows him breaking up the 'Great Society'

◄ **Source B:** President Lyndon Johnson in conversation the Tom Fletcher family of Inez, Kentucky in 1964. Fletcher was an unemployed saw mill worker and the Fletcher family of eight children earned only US$400 a year

ACTIVITIES

1. What can you learn from Source B about President Johnson?
2. What is the message of Source C?
3. Draw a two-column table with the headings 'similarities' and 'differences'. Fill it in to show the similarities and differences between the opposition to the policies of Kennedy and Johnson.

Practice questions

1. Explain why some American people opposed Johnson's Great Society programme. *(For guidance, see page 112.)*
2. How far did Johnson's 'Great Society' programme improve the lives of the American people during the 1960s? *(For guidance, see page 109.)*

Nixon and Watergate

Richard Nixon was elected to Congress in 1950 and made a name for himself in the McCarthy anti-communist witch-hunts. These were campaigns against alleged communists in the US government and other institutions carried out by Senator Joseph McCarthy in the period 1950–54. Many of the accused were blacklisted or lost their jobs, though most did not in fact belong to the Communist Party. Nixon was narrowly defeated by Kennedy in the 1960 presidential election campaign but was successful in 1968 and again in 1972. However, on 8 August 1974, he was forced to resign as president because of the Watergate scandal, which began in 1972.

There was an irony about the scandal because Nixon taped all conversations in his office as a protective measure. The recorded tapes eventually showed his involvement in the Watergate scandal. In addition, television had been one of the great communication developments of the 1950s and 1960s in the USA and it helped to bring down a president when the Senate hearings were broadcast.

Events of the scandal

▲ **Source D:** A cartoon in the *Washington Post*, 1973 at the height of the Watergate scandal. The investigations about the scandal were held in the Senate and were broadcast on television

CREEP

In 1968, Richard Nixon, the Republican candidate, was elected president. In 1972 he would have to seek re-election. Concerned that he might not be re-elected, he set up CREEP – Committee to Re-Elect the President. It was encouraged to use whatever methods necessary to ensure his re-election with US$350,000 set aside for 'dirty tricks'.

The break-in

On 17 June 1972, five members of CREEP were arrested for breaking into the Watergate offices of the Democrat Party. It soon became obvious that they were not ordinary burglars but were there to plant bugging devices.

The trial of the burglars

In January 1973, the Watergate burglars went on trial and were all convicted. In March, James McCord, one of those convicted, claimed in court that there had been a White House cover-up. Again Nixon denied all knowledge of the break-in or cover-up. However, he did admit that two of his top advisers, Bob Haldeman and John Ehrlichman, had been involved. They resigned on 30 April 1973.

The *Washington Post* reporters

Two reporters from the *Washington Post*, Carl Bernstein and Bob Woodward, discovered that all five burglars were employed by CREEP and that the CREEP fund was controlled by the White House. Nixon strongly denied any involvement by himself and his advisers. Nixon won a landslide victory in the 1972 presidential election.

4 Political change, 1960–2000

Source E: From the White House tapes recorded by President Nixon on 21 March 1973. They describe attempts at a cover-up of the involvement of the White House

Dean: That's right. Plus there is a real problem in raising money. Mitchell has been working on raising money. He is one of the ones with the most to lose. But there is no denying the fact that the White House, in Ehrlichman and Haldeman, are involved in the early money decisions.

President: How much money do you need?

Dean: I would say these people are going to cost a million dollars over the next two years.

President: You could get a million dollars. You could get it in cash. I know where it could be gotten. But the question is who the hell would handle it. Any ideas?

ACTIVITIES

1. What is the message of Source D?
2. What can you learn from Source E about President Nixon?
3. Working in pairs, imagine you are editors of the *Washington Post*. Put together a series of headlines to cover the key events of the Watergate scandal.
4. You have just watched Nixon's resignation. Put together a mobile phone text message informing a friend of what you have seen. You may use 'text language'. Remember to keep it brief, in line with a typical text message.

Practice question

Explain why Nixon resigned as president.
(For guidance, see page 112.)

The Senate Committee

The investigation of a Senate Committee set up to investigate the scandal was televised between May and November 1973. It became increasingly obvious that White House officials had been involved. One of them, John Dean, claimed there had been a cover-up directed by Nixon.

The White House tapes

One White House aide told the Senate Committee that in 1971 Nixon had installed a tape-recording system in the White House and that all the president's conversations had been taped. After at first refusing to hand over the tapes, Nixon handed over seven of the nine tapes on 21 November 1973 but they had been heavily edited. One of them had eighteen minutes missing. Finally, on 30 April 1974, Nixon was made to hand over all the tapes, unedited. They showed that he had been involved in the dirty tricks campaign and had repeatedly lied throughout the investigation. The tapes also shocked the nation because of the foul language used. Any foul language was indicated by the words 'expletive deleted' which occurred at regular intervals.

Nixon resigns

In July 1974, Congress decided to impeach Nixon. This meant that he would be put on trial with the Senate acting as the jury. On 8 August 1974, Nixon resigned, giving his reasons in a televised broadcast, to avoid **impeachment**. His successor, Gerald Ford, issued a decree in September of that year pardoning Nixon for any criminal acts that he had taken part in.

Effects of the scandal

Attitude to politicians

The scandal greatly undermined people's confidence in politics and politicians. In 1976 American people voted for the presidential election candidate they believed they could trust, Jimmy Carter, who promised never to lie. Even now scandals are generally given the nickname 'gate' after the name of the scandal. One example is the Irangate scandal of 1987.

Nixon's reputation

It utterly destroyed Nixon's reputation. He was seen as untrustworthy and was given the nickname of 'Tricky Dicky'. For many years afterwards the Watergate scandal overshadowed all his other achievements. Some 31 of Nixon's advisers went to prison for Watergate-related offences.

US Constitution

The Watergate scandal seemed to show how well the legal and political systems worked, as Nixon had been found out and forced to resign. Moreover, the balances of the US Constitution worked well. The Supreme Court had carried out its ultimate function and kept a check on the position of the president.

Reputation abroad

The scandal damaged the reputation of the USA abroad and made the USA a laughing stock. The USSR was able to use it as an example of the corruption of the capitalist system. The scandal came, also, at the same time as US troops were being withdrawn from Vietnam, an action that further undermined American self-confidence.

The powers of government

The powers of government were reduced by a series of measures including the:
- Election Campaign Act 1974 which set limits on election contributions to prevent corruption
- War Powers Act 1973 which required the president to consult Congress before sending American troops into combat
- Privacy Act 1974 which allowed citizens to have access to any files that the government may have had on them
- Congressional Budget Act 1974, which meant that the president could not use government money for his/her own purposes.

ACTIVITIES

1. Put together your own concept map showing the effects of the Watergate scandal. Rank order these effects clockwise, beginning with the most important at 12 o'clock.
2. How did the Watergate scandal affect the reputation of President Nixon?

Practice question

Explain why the Watergate Scandal was a turning point in the politics of the USA in the 1970s. *(For guidance, see page 112.)*

The Reagan years

Ronald Reagan, a former film star, won the presidential election campaign of 1980, defeating Jimmy Carter who had served only one term as president from 1977 to 1981. Reagan served two terms as president, from 1981 to 1989.

'Reaganomics'

Reagan inherited serious economic problems.

- By 1980 the world recession was biting deeply, bringing factory closures, rising unemployment (to 7.5 per cent) and oil shortages.
- Inflation had risen to nearly 15 per cent and budget deficits remained high.

Reagan's economic policies, known as Reaganomics, were based on the works of economist Arthur Laffer who argued that cutting taxes for businesses and the wealthier quarter of American citizens would encourage spending and put more money into the economy as a whole. The money would then eventually 'trickle down' or find its way into the middle and lower classes of American people, making everyone better off. Reagan reasoned that if these tax cuts at the top of society could trickle down and make everyone richer, the government could stop many of its social welfare programmes involving transfers of payments to those in poverty. In order to carry out these policies Reagan:

- cut welfare programme spending by over US$20 billion a year in his first three years, including food stamp programmes and various programmes to assist struggling mothers and children
- slashed taxes – in 1981 the Economic Recovery Tax Act reduced taxes by US$33 billion, making it the largest tax cut in US history – but to a point where the government was barely collecting any income revenue
- Medicare (see page 56) benefits were cut, requiring the elderly to pay more for health care.

The effects of Reaganomics

- Without tax revenues, the government was unable to pay for the services it provided.
- Worse, even though Reagan dramatically reduced tax rates, he actually dramatically increased total government spending, particularly in the areas of defence, which nearly doubled between 1981 and 1987. The government was forced to borrow money each year and the national debt rose to its highest ever level at almost US$1 trillion. People in all sectors lost their jobs and inflation soared. Reagan had created a deficit which was greater than the deficits created by all the presidents in American history combined.
- In 1987 Congress, increasingly worried by the rapidly growing federal budget deficit, rejected Reagan's budget for increased defence spending.
- There was a severe stock market crash in 1987, one of the worst stock market crashes since the crash of 1929 (see page 6). This was mainly due to Reagan's economic policies, which meant that the USA had the largest trading deficit of any of the leading industrialised nations (when the trade balance was negative and the value of what the USA imported was more than the value of what they exported). At the same time the economy was beginning to slow down as industry moved into recession.

> **Source F:** Ronald Reagan speaking in 1981
>
> *We who live in free market societies believe that growth, prosperity and ultimately human fulfilment are created from the bottom up, not the government down. Only when the human spirit is allowed to invent, and create, only when individuals are given a personal stake in deciding economic policies … only then can societies remain economically alive, dynamic and free.*

ACTIVITIES

1. What can you learn from Source F about Reaganomics?
2. How useful is Source G as evidence of President Reagan's policies?

Practice question

Describe the policy of Reaganomics. *(For guidance, see page 108.)*

▲ **Source G:** President Reagan explaining his tax programme for US citizens, July 1981

Other policies under Reagan

The space programme

The year 1986 was a disastrous year for America's space programme.
- In January the space shuttle *Challenger* exploded only seconds after lift-off, killing all seven crew members.
- In April a Titan rocket, carrying secret military equipment, exploded immediately after lift-off.
- In May a Delta rocket failed.
- Moreover, the development of the 'Star Wars' programme (see page 99) had proved very expensive and a further drain on the economy.

These disasters delayed Reagan's plans to develop a permanent orbital space station.

The environment

Reagan suggested that some damage to the environment was the price to pay if the nation wanted companies to create jobs and strengthen the economy. In a 1985 public opinion poll, two-thirds of the respondents disagreed with Reagan's approach and said they would be willing to pay higher prices in return for tighter limits on pollution.

> **Practice question**
> How far did President Reagan's reform policies deal with the social and economic problems facing America during the late 1980s? *(For guidance, see page 109.)*

▼ Demonstration of AIDS activists in Washington, DC, against President Reagan and the American government

Civil rights

Reagan incurred the anger of many civil rights organisations when he made some comments about Martin Luther King when Congress was discussing whether to make King's birthday a national holiday. He opposed this and only voted for it after overwhelming approval in Congress.

Though many women supported Reagan in 1980, he lost some of their support when he opposed abortion and showed a lack of concern for gender issues.

Acquired immune deficiency syndrome (AIDS)

When HIV/AIDS struck the USA, there was no known cure, and by 1985, nearly 4,000 people had died because of the virus. In 1989, the US Centre for Disease Control reported more than 46,000 AIDS deaths and estimated that there were about 800,000 American people infected. Initially, Reagan had a dismissive attitude to the AIDS crisis but gradually changed his views. By 1989, the federal government was spending US$2.3 billion a year on research and AIDS prevention. Reagan was criticised by some for supporting research into AIDS and by others for being slow to combat the virus.

War on drugs

On 14 October 1982, President Ronald Reagan declared illicit drugs to be a threat to US national security and the term 'War on drugs' was later coined. In 1988, Reagan created the Office of National Drug Control Policy to co-ordinate drug-related policy throughout the government.

4 Political change, 1960–2000

Changes under Bush Senior and Clinton

George Bush Snr

In 1989, Vice President George H. Bush Snr succeeded Ronald Reagan as president. He was president for one term until 1993. He had a reputation as a safe pair of hands who was willing to continue with Reagan's domestic policies.

Bush faced the problem of what to do with deficits run up in the Reagan years. At US$220 billion in 1990, the deficit had grown to three times its size since 1980. During his election campaign Bush had promised to cut taxes. However, he was forced to go back on his word and increase **indirect taxes** as well as reduce the number of wealthy people exempt from tax. He had to agree to new taxes on the wealthy, a cut in military spending and increased taxes on luxury items. However, the budget deficit continued to rise to US$300 billion. The recession developed which reduced government income from taxation even further.

By the end of Bush's presidential term interest and inflation rates were the lowest in years and the unemployment rate reached 7.8 per cent, the highest since 1984. In September 1992, the Census Bureau reported that 14.2 per cent of all Americans lived in poverty.

President Bush Snr signed two significant pieces of domestic legislation during his tenure.

- The Americans with Disabilities Act 1990 (see Source H), which forbade discrimination based on disability in employment, public accommodations and transportation. This is considered to be the most important anti-discrimination legislation since the Civil Rights Acts of the 1960s.
- The Clean Air Act 1990 which built on previous legislation of 1963, 1970 and 1977. It focused on three aspects of clean air: reducing urban smog, curbing acid rain, and eliminating industrial emissions of toxic chemicals.

Bush was less successful in other areas.

- He had promised in his election campaign to tackle drug use as his top priority. He gave several billion dollars to the Drug Enforcement Agency which worked on employee drug testing and increased border controls, but this made little impact, especially on those suffering an addiction to cocaine and heroin.
- There were race riots in Los Angeles, Atlanta, Birmingham, Seattle and Chicago in 1992 following the arrest and beating of Rodney King, an African-American person who had been caught speeding by four white policemen. The incident was filmed on a home video camera by a local resident.

> **ACTIVITIES**
> 1. Why was Source H widely published in the USA?
> 2. Should George Bush Snr be regarded as a successful president?

◀ **Source H:** President Bush signing the Americans with Disabilities Act (ADA) 26 July, 1990

Change under Clinton

In 1992 Bill Clinton defeated George Bush Snr in the presidential election campaign. Clinton was a Democrat, representing the political opposite of his two Republican predecessors, Reagan and Bush Snr, with very different views on the economy and social welfare. The economic downturn was a major reason for his success in the presidential election. By 1992 the gap between the richest and poorest citizens in America had grown even wider, which only served to damage the stability of American society.

There were three major features of Clinton's domestic policies.

1 The move away from Reaganomics

Clinton was determined to reduce the budget deficit left by his predecessors while, at the same time, increasing federal government spending and investment in education and welfare.

- He was able to reduce the huge budget deficit left over from the Reagan era. By 1996 he had reduced the deficit to US$107 billion and by 1998 the budget was balanced for the first time since 1969.
- He was president during the longest period of sustained economic growth in the history of the USA. The value of the stock market had tripled, the unemployment rate was the lowest for almost 30 years and there was the highest level of home ownership in the history of the USA.
- The North American Free Trade Agreement was signed with Canada and Mexico, setting up a free trade area between the three countries and stimulating US export markets.
- More than 22 million jobs were created in less than eight years – the most ever under a single administration, and more than were created in the previous 12 years.
- Unemployment dropped from more than 7 per cent in 1993 to just 4.0 per cent in November 2000. Unemployment for African-American and Hispanic people fell to the lowest rates on record, and the rate for women was the lowest in more than 40 years.
- Interest rates were kept low and this made it possible for more families to buy homes. During Clinton's presidency, the homeownership rate increased from 64.2 per cent in 1992 to 67.7 per cent, the highest rate ever for the USA.

2 Important welfare and social reforms

To help parents succeed at work and at home, President Clinton signed the Family and Medical Leave Act in 1993. Over 20 million American people have taken unpaid leave to care for a newborn child or sick family member.

In 1996, Clinton introduced a minimum wage of US$4.75 an hour, which was increased to US$5.15 in May 1997. In 1993 he had failed in his ambitious attempt to introduce a system of universal health insurance. The Health Security Bill was attacked by the insurance industry and the American Medical Association and was rejected by Congress.

The Clinton Administration expanded efforts to provide mothers and newborn children with health care. By 2000, a record 82 per cent of all mothers received ante-natal care. The infant mortality rate dropped from 8.5 deaths per 1,000 in 1992 to 7.2 deaths per 1,000 in 1998, the lowest rate ever recorded in the USA.

3 A series of scandals

Clinton was linked to the Whitewater scandal of 1996 when two of his former business associates were convicted of multiple fraud over a housing development in the Whitewater area of Arkansas. Although it dragged on for several years, no conclusive evidence was ever found of illegal dealings by Clinton and his wife Hillary.

However, Kenneth Starr, the man leading the Whitewater enquiry, did find proof that Clinton had been having an affair with Monica Lewinsky, a member of the White House staff. Having repeatedly denied any such affair, Clinton was forced to make a public apology to the American people. Many people felt that the support of his wife enabled him to continue as president. He was impeached by the House of Representatives in December 1998, on the grounds of perjury and obstruction of justice, but in 1999 the Senate acquitted him of impeachment charges. Again, Clinton apologised to the nation, saying he was 'profoundly sorry' for his actions (Source I).

> **Source I:** Part of President Clinton's televised speech to the US nation, 17 August 1998
>
> *Indeed, I did have a relationship with Ms. Lewinsky that was not appropriate. In fact, it was wrong. It constituted a critical lapse in judgement and a personal failure on my part for which I am solely and completely responsible.*
>
> *But I told the grand jury today and I say to you now that at no time did I ask anyone to lie, to hide or destroy evidence or to take any other unlawful action. I know that my public comments and my silence about this matter gave a false impression. I misled people, including even my wife. I deeply regret that.*
>
> *This has gone on too long, cost too much and hurt too many innocent people. Now, this matter is between me, the two people I love most – my wife and our daughter – and our God. I must put it right, and I am prepared to do whatever it takes to do so.*

ACTIVITIES

1. How successful was President Clinton in reviving the US economy?
2. Study Sources I and J. Suggest reasons why President Clinton thought it necessary to address the Senate and the US nation.
3. Use Source I and your own knowledge to explain why there was a scandal over Clinton's relationship with Monica Lewinsky.
4. Make a copy of the following table and summarise the successes and failures of the domestic policies of the three presidents.

	Successes	Failures
Reagan		
Bush Snr		
Clinton		

▲ **Source J:** 'Profoundly sorry' President Clinton makes a short statement after the Senate had acquitted him of impeachment charges at the White House, 12 February 1999

Practice question

How far did President Clinton's policies change the economic situation in the USA during the 1990s?
(For guidance, see page 109.)

5 Social change, 1950–2000

There were fundamental changes in US society in the second half of the twentieth century. Although the cinema was still important, it was television, popular music and later the internet which had the greatest impact, especially on the young. The 1950s saw the emergence of the teenager and a new and ever changing youth culture followed by the student protests and hippy movement of the 1960s. There were also important developments in the position of women in US society, influenced by the Second World War and the feminist movement of the 1960s and 1970s.

Changes in music, entertainment, media and literature

▲ **Source A:** Elvis Presley

Popular culture in the second half of the twentieth century in the USA was greatly influenced by the music, cinema, literature, the popularity of television and the emergence of the computer and internet.

Music

1950s

The 1950s witnessed the birth of rock and roll music. This gave teenagers music of their own to listen to, instead of having to listen to their parents' type of music. The more parents disliked the new music, the more popular it was with teenagers. In 1956, Elvis Presley erupted onto the pop music scene, singing songs that broke all sales records, such as 'Heartbreak Hotel' and 'Hound Dog' (Source A). He was a phenomenal success with teenagers, while their parents and teachers deplored his sensual style of performing, his tight jeans and his permanent sneer. He was the first rock and roll star to influence the young in their attitude to authority and their appearance. Moreover, he greatly popularised rock and roll music. Rock and roll grew and was transformed into many musical variations in the following decades.

1960s

In the 1960s the Beatles, the Rolling Stones and other British groups took the USA by storm. 'Hard rock' grew popular, and protest songs, such as those by singer/songwriter Bob Dylan, became common. The Beach Boys were an American rock band, formed in 1961, who gained popularity for their close vocal harmonies and lyrics reflecting a southern California youth culture of cars, surfing and romance (Source B). Many white middle-class parents were shocked and concerned by their teenage children's explosion of anger and lack of respect for the law, and believed rock and roll music encouraged teenage crime.

1970–2000

Popular music underwent many changes in the later twentieth century and was a key factor in influencing the culture of young American people.

- In the 1970s disco performers such as Donna Summer, the Bee Gees, KC and the Sunshine Band, Chic, and the Jacksons became very popular. Disco was a reaction to the domination of rock music and was particularly popular with women. The disco became a favourite hang-out for teenagers, further popularised by the film *Saturday Night Fever* (1977).
- Heavy metal music also became popular. Heavy metal bands such as Led Zeppelin, Black Sabbath and Deep Purple led the way, followed by Motörhead and Iron Maiden. Their music was characterised by amplifier distortion and long guitar solos.
- There were influential solo artists such as Bruce Springsteen and John Mellencamp. Springsteen became very popular due to the fact his music focused on the struggles of 'ordinary' people, more especially the working class. His albums such as *Born to Run* (1975) and *Born in the USA* (1984) were based on his own experiences of life in New Jersey. John Mellencamp rose to stardom in the 1980s with a string of Top 10 singles. In a similar fashion to Springstein, Mellenchamp wrote about everyday life. He also helped to set up Farm Aid and organised a concert to try to prevent families from losing farm land.
- Rap and hip hop music developed, to a certain extent, from the disco music of the 1970s and became very popular in the last 20 years of the century. Although very much a product of inner-city areas, especially those with high unemployment among young black American people, research carried out on consumer groups during the mid-1990s highlighted the fact that over 75 per cent of hip hop record buyers were young and white. Hip hop had become popular and mainstream. Jay-Z's *Vol. 2 … Hard Knock Life* album reached the US number 1 position for 5 weeks in 1998. Other artists/bands such as Ice-T, Will Smith and the Fugees all achieved great chart success.

▲ **Source B:** The Beach Boys, one of the most popular 1960s rock groups in America

ACTIVITIES

1. Study Sources A, B and C. How far do these photos reflect the changes in popular music in the years 1950–2000?
2. Working in pairs, put together a timeline for the period 1950–2000 to show the key changes in music.

Practice question

Describe the developments in popular music between 1970 and 2000. *(For guidance, see page 108.)*

▲ **Source C:** Jay-Z in concert

Entertainment: The cinema

The cinema was popular, but less so than in the inter-war years of 1918–39 because of the growing influence of television. Average weekly cinema attendances fell from 90 million a week in 1946 to 47 million ten years later.

Drive-ins

The drive-in cinema, first opened in the 1930s, became very popular in the 1950s and early 1960s, particularly in rural areas, with some 4,000 drive-ins spreading across the USA. Among its advantages was the fact that a family with a baby could take care of their child while watching a movie, while teenagers with access to cars found drive-ins ideal for dates. In the 1950s, the greater privacy afforded to patrons gave drive-ins a reputation as immoral, and they were labelled 'passion pits' in the media.

Multiplexes

Stanley H. Durwood became the father of the multiplex movie theatre in 1963 when he opened the first ever mall multiplex, made up of two side-by-side theatres with 700 seats, at Ward Parkway Center in Kansas City.

Anti-heroes

In the period following the Second World War young people wanted new and exciting symbols of rebellion. Hollywood responded to audience demands; the late 1940s and 1950s saw the rise of the anti-hero, a main character who has a lack of traditional heroic qualities, such as idealism or courage. Newcomers like James Dean (see page 72), Paul Newman and Marlon Brando replaced more traditional actors like Bette Davis, James Cagney, Tyrone Power, Van Johnson and Robert Taylor. In later decades, this new generation of method actors would be followed by Robert De Niro, Jack Nicholson and Al Pacino. Anti-heroines included Ava Gardner, Kim Novak and Marilyn Monroe – an exciting, vibrant, sexy star.

Blockbusters

The 1970s saw the emergence of the blockbuster film, headed up by *Jaws* (1975), directed by the 27-year-old Steven Spielberg. This became the highest grossing film in history – until *Star Wars* two years later, which was directed by George Lucas.

Following this model, Hollywood continued to search in the 1980s for the one large 'event film' that everyone, including international audiences, wanted to see. These films had dazzling special effects technology, sophisticated soundtracks, and costly, highly-paid stars. Spielberg followed *Jaws* with *ET* (1982) and teamed up with Lucas for the *Indiana Jones* films of the 1980s, the first of which, *Raiders of the Lost Ark* (1981), made a household name out of the lead actor, Harrison Ford. The video recorder (VCR) encouraged film hire and home viewing and was a further stimulus to the film industry.

1990s

In the 1990s, for the most part, cinema attendance was up – mostly at multiplexes throughout the country. It was the decade of the mega-paid movie stars such as Arnold Schwarzenegger, Tom Cruise, Sylvester Stallone, Mel Gibson, Eddie Murphy, Kevin Costner, Harrison Ford, Robin Williams, Jim Carrey, Demi Moore and Julia Roberts. The VCR was still popular in most households (about three-quarters of them had VCRs in 1991) and rentals and purchase of films on videotape were big business – much larger than sales of movie tickets. By 1997, the first DVDs (digital video discs) had emerged in stores, featuring sharper resolution and better quality pictures. Films such as *Jurassic Park* (1993) and *Star Wars Episode I – The Phantom Menace* (1999) used ever more advanced digital imagery and special effects.

> **ACTIVITY**
>
> Put together a mind map summarising the main developments in the cinema in the years 1950–2000.

5 Social change, 1950–2000

Television

During the 1940s, there were relatively few television sets in American homes. However, the number of televisions increased from 7,000 in 1946 to 50 million by 1960. Between 1959 and 1970, the percentage of households in the USA with at least one television went from 88 per cent to 96 per cent. Some called television an invention for stupid people to watch. By the end of the 1950s, however, television was here to stay. The average family watched 6 hours a day. Subscription television (such as cable and satellite) became popular in the early 1980s, and has been growing in significance since then.

American people especially liked games shows and funny shows with comedians such as Milton Berle and Lucille Ball. They also liked shows that offered a mix of entertainment, such as those presented by Arthur Godfrey and Ed Sullivan. The 'Western' became one of the most popular styles of programme, with popular series including *The Lone Ranger* (see Source D), *Bonanza* and *Gunsmoke*. These gave an idealised image of the American West of the nineteenth century.

People from other countries watching American television in the 1950s might have thought that all American people were white Christians. It celebrated traditional American values. Popular programmes such as *I Love Lucy* and *The Honeymooners* gave a romanticised view of American middle-class suburban life. In a sense, early television created its own view of American culture.

What was portrayed on television came to be accepted as normal. The ideal family, the ideal schools and neighbourhoods, the world, were all seen in a way which had only a partial basis in reality. People began to accept what was heard and seen on television because they were 'eye witnesses' to events as never before. Programmes such as *You Are There* brought historical events into the living rooms of many American people. At the same time, television failed to recognise that America was a great mix of races and religions. Few members of racial or religious minorities were represented on television. Those who did appear were usually shown to be working for white people.

Soap operas

American soap operas became, and still are, very popular. Long-running daytime dramas included *Search for Tomorrow* (1951–86), *Love of Life* (1951–80), *The Doctors* (1963–82), *Dallas* (1978–91), *Dynasty* (1981–89) and *Beverly Hills 90210* (1990–2000).

Chat shows

Daytime chat shows such as *Phil Donahue* (1970–96) and *The Jerry Springer Show* (1991–present) have also pulled in many viewers. By far the most successful of these has been the *Oprah Winfrey Show* (often simply referred to as *Oprah* or just *O*) which is the longest-running daytime television chat show in the USA, having run nationally since 8 September 1986. It has featured book clubs, celebrity interviews and self-improvement segments.

> **ACTIVITY**
>
> Study Source D. What image does this give of the American West?

> **Practice question**
>
> Explain why television had so much influence on US society in the 1950s and 1960s. *(For guidance, see page 112.)*

◀ **Source D:** A scene from the popular television Western of the 1950s, *The Lone Ranger*

Developments in information technology

Information technology began to have a significant impact on American society in the 1990s.

Personal computers

The 1990s saw a massive growth in the sale of personal computers. This was due mainly to the competition between two rival organisations, Microsoft and Apple.

- Bill Gates set up his company Microsoft in 1975. Microsoft launched its first retail version of Microsoft Windows on 20 November 1985. Gates and Microsoft came to dominate the development of computer electronics, computer software and personal computers.
- The major rival was Apple Computer, Inc. which was set up by Steve Jobs, Steve Wozniak and Ronald Wayne in California in 1976. The company's best-known hardware products included the Macintosh computers.

The internet

Another major development of the 1990s was the internet.

- In 1991, the first really user-friendly interface to the internet was developed at the University of Minnesota.
- In the following year, Delphi was the first national commercial online service to offer internet access to its subscribers.
- The release of Windows 98 in June 1998 with the Microsoft browser integrated into the desktop enabled Bill Gates to take advantage of the enormous growth of the internet.

▲ **Source E:** The first Apple computer built by Steve Jobs and Steve Wozniak back in 1976

Gaming

The development of computer generated games became a very significant pastime for the younger generation.

- The first commercially viable video game was *Computer Space* in 1971. In subsequent decades there was massive growth in computer games as well as significant improvements in technology.
- In the 1980s Nintendo introduced the first modern game console called the NES (Nintendo Entertainment System), followed by others such as the Sega Mega Drive, the Sony PlayStation and, in 2001, the Microsoft Xbox.

Impact on US society

These technological developments transformed US society in the last decade of the twentieth century.

- The internet had a drastic impact on culture and commerce. This included the rise of near instant communication by electronic mail (email), text-based discussion forums and e-commerce.
- More and more leisure time for the younger generation began to be taken up with social networking on the internet as well as the various game consoles. This led to increasing concern for a generation abandoning an active lifestyle for passive activities, resulting in lack of exercise and obesity issues.

> ### ACTIVITIES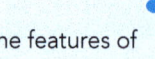
>
> 1. What can you learn from Source E about the features of the first Apple computer?
> 2. How important were the computer and internet in bringing change to US society in the later twentieth century?

> ### Practice question
>
> The lives of many American people during the period 1960 to 2000 were influenced by developments such as:
>
> - the cinema
> - television
> - information technology.
>
> Arrange these developments in order of their significance in influencing the lives of American people during this period. *(For guidance, see pages 110–11.)*

Literature

There were two major features of American literature in the second half of the twentieth century: the continued search for the 'great American novel' and counter-cultural literary works, which challenged the general conservatism of US society.

The great American novel

This was the quest to write a novel which defined the meaning of being 'American', linking this to the history of the nation and the diverse nature of US society. It built on the work of pre-Second World War novelists such as Ernest Hemingway with novels such as *The Sun Also Rises* and *A Farewell to Arms* and F. Scott Fitzgerald's *The Great Gatsby*.

The quest for the 'great American novel' led to the publication of some of the most popular works in American literary history in the 30 years after the end of the Second World War and included:

- *To Kill a Mockingbird* by Harper Lee – published in 1960, it focused on issues of racial inequality and rape
- *The Catcher in the Rye* by J. D. Salinger – published in 1951, the book commented on the apparent madness of American society, especially with teenagers
- *Rabbit, Run* by John Updike – published in 1960, focused on changes in middle-class American society
- Norman Mailer's popular novel, *The Naked and the Dead*, published in 1948, focused on the Second World War and Mailer's own experiences of fighting in the war in the Pacific, more especially the Philippines.
- Cormac McCarthy's epic novel *Blood Meridian*, which was published in 1985, focusing on the American West, is one of the most highly acclaimed American novels of the later twentieth century and built on the work of William Faulkner.

Counterculture

Another major theme in the development of American literature in the years after the Second World War was counterculture which challenged the traditional conservatism of American society. Salinger's *The Catcher in the Rye* focused on the theme of teenage rebellion in US society.

The 'Beat Generation', often referred to as the Beat or Beatniks, were a group of novelists and poets who led the way in rebelling against conservative values. Allen Ginsberg led the way with his poem *Howl* published in 1956 which was so sexually explicit that it shocked contemporary American society. This was followed by Jack Kerouac *On the Road*, published in 1957 and William S. Burroughs' *Naked Lunch*, published two years later, which both focused on the controversial issue of hard drugs. This theme is taken up by Hunter S. Thompson in his novel *Fear and Loathing in Las Vegas* (1971) with its graphic descriptions of drug taking.

Betty Friedan's *The Feminine Mystique* published in 1963 challenged the traditional role of women in American society and did much to encourage the re-emergence of the Women's Liberation Movement (see page 79).

African-American authors focused on racial inequality in American society, such as Ralph Ellison who in his novel, *Invisible Man*, published in 1952, highlighted racial tension in the North. Richard Wright's *Black Boy* drew on the author's own experiences of segregated education in the South. It was written in 1945 but not published until 1971 because of Wright's involvement with the Communist Party. Toni Morrison won the Novel Prize for Literature with her controversial debut novel, *The Bluest Eye*, published in 1970, using the theme of rape to comment on racial inequalities in American society. Her novel of 1985, *Beloved*, focuses on slavery and the plight of a slave who escapes during the American Civil War of 1861–65.

> **ACTIVITY**
>
> Working in pairs, carry out further research on one of the literary works mentioned in this section, more especially its key themes and impact on American society.

> **Practice question**
>
> How far did literature influence life in America between 1950 and 2000? *(For guidance, see page 109.)*

Changes in youth culture

Possibly the greatest social change in the USA of the 1950s and the 1960s was the emergence of a distinct youth culture.

1950s

The decade saw the emergence of the teenager and teenage rebellion. In the past young adults had simply imitated their parents' tastes and fashions and had been firmly kept in their place. The teenager of the 1950s seemed to want to rebel against everything and especially against whatever their parents believed in. Some formed gangs, cruised in cars, drank heavily and attacked property.

In addition they developed their own identity as teenagers by wearing distinctive clothes and listening to their own music. Other young people 'dropped out' of conventional society altogether to become beatniks.

These changes were due to several factors.

- Young people in 1950s America had far more money to spend than previous generations of young people due to the country's increasing affluence, and companies responded with new products specifically targeted towards them. In 1957, it was estimated that the average teenager had US$10–15 a week to spend, compared with US$1–2 in the 1940s. Teenagers' annual spending power climbed from US$10 billion in 1950 to US$25 billion in 1959.
- They were the first generation to grow up under the shadow of nuclear war – it was a fear that nuclear weapons would destroy the world at the push of a button. The world could end at any time so teenagers wanted to enjoy 'today'.
- Many teenagers were influenced by the youth films of the 1950s. *Rebel Without a Cause* was the first film to appeal specifically to a teenage audience. As such, it was also the first film to address the issue of a **generation gap**. The film made a cult hero of James Dean, the more so as he was killed in a car accident in 1955 aged only 24. In the film, Dean plays a character who rebels against his parents, even coming to blows with his father, and gets into trouble with the local police for drunkenness.

ACTIVITY

What can you learn from Source F about attitudes towards teenagers in the 1950s?

Practice question

Explain why many teenagers rebelled against society in the 1950s. *(For guidance, see page 112.)*

▲ **Source F:** A poster advertising the film *Rebel Without a Cause*

Youth counterculture

The American youth continued to develop their own counterculture during the late 1950s and 1960s.

- Hair was grown longer and beards became common. Blue jeans and T-shirts took the place of slacks, jackets, and ties.
- The use of illegal drugs increased.
- The introduction of the contraceptive pill seemed to encourage greater sexual freedom and promiscuity.

The hippy movement

Other young people protested in a totally different way. They decided to 'drop out' of society and become hippies. This meant they grew their hair long, wore distinctive clothes and developed an 'alternative lifestyle'. Often they travelled round the country in buses and vans and wore flowers in their hair as a symbol of peace rather than war. Their slogan was 'Make love, not war.'

Because hippies often wore flowers and handed them out to police they were called 'flower children'. They often settled in communes. San Francisco became the hippy capital of America. Their behaviour, especially their use of drugs, frequently led to clashes with the police.

They were influenced by rock groups such as the Grateful Dead and the Doors (Source G). The high point of the movement came at the Woodstock rock concert at the end of the 1960s (Source H). Woodstock was a 3-day music festival in rural New York State in August 1969 attended by almost half a million people. The festival gave its name to the era, the Woodstock Generation.

This movement was of particular concern to the older generation because:

- hippies often refused to work
- they experimented in drugs such as marijuana and LSD
- many were from middle-class and not under-privileged backgrounds; they rejected all the values that their parents believed in.

> **Source G:** Jim Morrison, lead singer of the group the Doors, 1969
>
> *I like ideas about the breaking away or overthrowing of established order. I am interested in anything about revolt, disorder, chaos, especially activity that seems to have no meaning. It seems to me to be the road towards freedom – external freedom is a way to bring about internal freedom.*

ACTIVITIES

1. What does Source G tell you about youth counterculture?
2. What can you learn about the hippy culture from Source H?

Practice questions

1. Explain why youth culture changed between the 1950s and 1960s. *(For guidance, see page 112.)*
2. Describe the youth counterculture of the 1960s. *(For guidance, see page 108.)*

Source H: A group of hippies wearing typical 'hippy' clothes, drumming together before the start of the Woodstock festival in 1969

Student protest

In the 1960s students became heavily involved in the civil rights movement and the campaign for greater freedom of speech at universities, while many opposed US involvement in the conflict in Vietnam.

The swinging sixties
The attitudes of teenagers in the 1950s carried over to the next decade. It is often described as the 'swinging' sixties as the young distanced themselves even more from the older generation and its view of how the young should behave. They demanded greater freedom in everything they did: the music they listened to; the clothes they wore; the social life they led.

Protest singers
The 1960s saw an explosion in pop music which, in turn, was an expression of this emerging youth culture and of protest against important issues of the day. For example, Bob Dylan's lyrics covered the themes of the changing times – nuclear war, racism and the hypocrisy of waging war. Artists such as Jimi Hendrix, Janis Joplin and Joan Baez sang about sex, drugs and opposition to the war in Vietnam.

Universities
Many students wanted a greater say in their own education. They wanted to take part in running the universities and an end to college rules and restrictions imposed upon them. The 1960s were also a time of student protest across the world. For example, in the later 1960s there were student protests in Northern Ireland for civil rights for Catholics and in 1968 student demonstrations and strikes in Paris.

The Students for a Democratic Society
One of the first student protest groups to emerge in the USA was the Students for a Democratic Society (SDS). It was set up in 1959 by Tom Hayden to give students a greater say in how courses and universities should be run. It had 100,000 members by the end of the 1960s. The SDS first achieved national prominence when, in 1964, it helped to organise the 'free speech movement' in the University of California at Berkeley. Up to half of Berkeley's 27,500 students took part in this campaign in 1964 and 1965. The SDS also played a key role in the protest movement against the war in Vietnam, including staging draft card burnings.

The influence of Martin Luther King
For many young American people, white and black, their first experience of protest was in civil rights. Martin Luther King's methods proved inspirational and many white students supported the freedom marches, freedom rides and the sit-ins of the early and mid-1960s (see pages 38–39). Moreover, a disproportionate number of black American students were called up to fight in Vietnam. Influential black figures such as Martin Luther King spoke out against the war.

Involvement with civil rights
In 1964, student societies organised rallies and marches to support the civil rights campaign. Many were appalled at the racism in American society and were determined to expose racists in their own colleges: they demanded free speech.

The conflict in Vietnam
Many students were called up to the armed forces. This was known as the draft system. Opposition to the war grew with the number of casualties. In 1965 there were fewer than 2,000 US casualties. By 1968 the number had increased to 14,000. Some students questioned the right of the USA to be in Vietnam. The USA was supporting a corrupt regime in South Vietnam. US methods of warfare brought even greater opposition, especially the use of chemical weapons such as napalm and the killing of innocent civilians such as at My Lai in 1968.

Anti-war protests
The anti-war protests reached their peak during 1968–70. In the first half of 1968, there were over 100 demonstrations against the war, involving 400,000 students. In 1969, 700,000 people marched in Washington DC against the war. Students at these demonstrations often burned draft cards or, more seriously, the US flag which was a criminal offence. This, in turn, led to angry clashes with police. However, the most serious clash took place at Kent State University, Ohio, on 4 May 1970 (Sources I and J). President Nixon showed little sympathy for student opposition as shown in his speech (Source K). National guardsmen, called to disperse the students, used tear gas to try to move them. When they refused to move shots were fired. Four people were killed and 11 injured. The press in the USA and abroad were horrified and some 400 colleges were closed as 2 million students went on strike in protest against this action.

◀ **Source I:** A shocked student holds her head in disbelief as she looks at the body of one of the four students killed at Kent State University, Ohio, in 1970

Source J: Arthur Krause, the father of one of the students who died at Kent State University, talking about his daughter on television, 5 May 1970

She resented being called a bum because she disagreed with someone else's opinion. She felt that our crossing into Cambodia was wrong. Is this dissent a crime? Is this a reason for killing her? Have we come to such a state in this country that a young girl has to be shot because she disagrees deeply with the action of her government?

Source K: Part of President Richard Nixon's speech, 1 May 1970

You think of those kids out there [in Vietnam]. They are the greatest. You see these bums blowing up the campuses ... they are the luckiest people in the world, going to the greatest universities and here they are burning up the books, I mean storming around about this issue – get rid of the war. Out there [in Vietnam] we've got kids who are just doing their duty. They stand tall and they are proud.

The importance of the student movement

In many respects, the most long-lasting achievement of the student movement was youth culture itself. By the end of the 1960s, there were profound changes in the whole lifestyle of the young. This was partly reflected in fashion, with the young becoming far more fashion-conscious and determined to move away from the 'norm' of the older generation. Perhaps the best example of this is the miniskirt, which was also a reflection of the greater sexual permissiveness of the era. Teenagers became much more aware of their individuality and demanded a greater say in what they wore and did.

Although the SDS and student protests did not bring an end to the war in Vietnam, there is no doubt that they helped to force a shift in government policy and make the withdrawal from Vietnam much more likely. They certainly influenced President Johnson's decision not to seek re-election in 1968.

In addition, the student movement provided greater publicity for the racism still prevalent in US society. The support of many white students for black civil rights strengthened the whole protest movement and showed that most American youths would no longer tolerate discrimination and segregation.

Finally, it should be remembered that the bulk of the students were of middle-class origin. They would have been expected to support the government in most areas. For such people to oppose the government on key issues (and in some cases oppose their families' views) was virtually unheard of and shook the older, more conservative generation.

ACTIVITIES

1. Make your own mind map to show the reasons behind student protest
   - Rank in order the reasons clockwise from the most to the least important.
   - Use different coloured pens to show links between some of the reasons.
   - Briefly explain the links between the reasons.
2. Put together a headline in a national newspaper the day after the Kent State University deaths.
3. What can you learn from Sources I and J about the Kent State University shootings?

Practice question

How far was student protest responsible for the development of an anti-war movement in America? *(For guidance, see page 109.)*

The changing role of women

There were important changes in the position of women in US society in the second half of the twentieth century.

The impact of the Second World War

Before 1945, most American women had 'traditional' roles as wives and mothers, with few women following careers. There were few real career opportunities except in typically 'female' professions such as teaching, nursing and secretarial work.

The Second World War had mixed results for the position of women.

- Women made a great contribution to the war effort and this opened up many new areas of employment for working-class women, especially in producing munitions. Indeed, the pay in munitions work was much higher than that normally paid to women in typically 'female' occupations. The number of women employed increased from 12 million in 1940 to 18.5 million, five years later. Many of these new jobs were in traditionally 'male' occupations such as the shipyards, aircraft factories and munitions.
- Women also joined the armed forces, with about 300,000 serving in the women's sections of the army, navy and the nursing corps.

Nevertheless, at the end of the war:

- the majority of women willingly gave up their wartime jobs and returned to their role as mothers and wives and their traditional 'female' jobs
- women were generally excluded from the highest, well-paid jobs and, on average, earned 50–60 per cent of the wage that men earned for doing the same job
- women could still be dismissed from their job when they married.

ACTIVITY

What can you learn from Source L about the role of women during the Second World War?

Practice question

Explain why the Second World War was a turning point for women. *(For guidance, see page 112.)*

◀ **Source L:** A poster from wartime USA featuring Rosie the Riveter, 1942. Rosie was a fictional female worker used by the US government in a poster campaign to encourage women to help with the war effort. Hollywood even made a movie about Rosie

1950s

The Second World War had seen some progress in the position of women but, for the most part, this did not continue for the generation of women who followed. Indeed, there was much media influence encouraging women to adopt their 'traditional' family role (Sources M, N and O). Women who went out to work instead of getting married were treated with great suspicion by the rest of society.

In the 1950s, growing numbers of women, especially those from middle-class backgrounds, began to challenge their traditional role as they became increasingly frustrated with life as a housewife. Moreover, the contraceptive pill gave females much greater choice about when or whether to have children. This could be prevented or postponed whilst a woman pursued her career.

Women were now much better educated so they could have a professional career. In 1950, there were 721,000 women at university. By 1960, this had reached 1.3 million. Moreover, the impact of labour-saving devices and convenience foods gave women more free time and this led some to seek paid employment. However, many of these women had a very limited choice of career because, once they married, they were expected to devote their energies to their husband and children.

Source M: From *The Woman's Guide to Better Living*, written in the 1950s

Whether you are a man or woman, the family is the unit to which you most genuinely belong. The family is the centre of your living. If it isn't, you've gone astray.

Source O: From the 1955 film *The Tender Trap*. A conversation between two of the leading characters in the film, Debbie Reynolds and Frank Sinatra

Reynolds: The theatre's all right, but it's only temporary.

Sinatra: Are you thinking of something else?

Reynolds: Marriage, I hope. A career is just fine, but it's no substitute for marriage. Don't you think a man is just the most important thing in the world? A woman isn't a woman until she's been married and had children.

ACTIVITIES

1. Study Source M. What view does it have about the role of women?
2. How far is the view in Source M confirmed by Sources N and O?

◀ **Source N:** The typical 'mother' image from the 1950s

1960s

Despite post-war attitudes, the number of women in employment continued to increase as they were a valuable source of cheap, often part-time, labour for many employers. In 1950, women made up nearly 29 per cent of the workforce. By 1960, this was almost 50 per cent. Eleanor Roosevelt, the widow of President Roosevelt, made an important contribution to the cause when, in 1960, she set up a commission to investigate the status of women at work. Eleanor had been a keen supporter of women's rights since the 1920s. The report was published in 1963 and highlighted women's second-class status in employment. For example, 95 per cent of company managers and 85 per cent of technical workers were men. Only 7 per cent of doctors were women and even less, 4 per cent, were lawyers. Women earned only 50 to 60 per cent of the wages of men who did the same job and they generally held low-paid jobs.

Betty Friedan

Another woman, Betty Friedan, was even more influential in the emergence of the women's movement. As we have already seen on page 71, her book, *The Feminine Mystique* (1963) expressed the thoughts of many women – that there was more to life than being a mother and housewife. Indeed, the expression 'the feminine mystique' was her term for the idea that a woman's happiness was all tied up with her domestic role.

Friedan was important because she encouraged women to reject this 'mystique' and called for progress in female employment opportunities. Disillusioned with the lack of progress in employment opportunities despite government legislation in 1963 and 1964 (see page 56), in 1966 she set up the National Organisation for Women (NOW).

> **Source P:** From *The Feminine Mystique* by Betty Friedan, 1963
>
> *The problem lay buried, unspoken for many years in the minds of American women. It was a strange stirring, a sense of dissatisfaction, a yearning that women suffered in the middle of the twentieth century in the United States.*

National Organisation for Women (NOW)

NOW was set up by mainly white middle-class women in order to attack obvious examples of discrimination. By the early 1970s it had 40,000 members and had organised demonstrations in many American cities. Its members challenged discrimination in the courts and in a series of cases between 1966 and 1971 secured US$30 million in back pay owed to women who had not been paid wages equal to men.

> **Source Q:** The Bill of Rights which was agreed at NOW's first national conference, 1967
>
> 1. Equal Rights Constitution Amendment
> 2. Enforce Law Banning Sex Discrimination in Employment
> 3. Maternity Leave Rights in Employment and Social Security Benefits
> 4. Tax Deduction for Home and Child Care Expenses for Working Parents
> 5. Child Day Care Centres
> 6. Equal and Unsegregated Education
> 7. Equal Job Training Opportunities and Allowances for Women in Poverty
> 8. The Right of Women to Control Their Reproductive Lives

ACTIVITIES

1. Working in pairs, write letters to a local newspaper from two American women who have read Betty Friedan's *The Feminine Mystique* in the mid-1960s:
   - ☐ one giving reasons in support of Friedan's views
   - ☐ one opposing them and giving the 'traditional' view of women.
2. Study Source Q. Which do you think are the **three** most important aims of NOW? Give reasons for your choices.

Practice question

How far had attitudes towards the role and status of women changed by the 1960s? *(For guidance, see page 79.)*

5 Social change, 1950–2000

The Women's Liberation Movement

The Women's Liberation Movement was the name given to women who had far more radical aims than NOW. They were also known as **feminists** and were much more active in challenging discrimination. Indeed, the really extreme feminists wanted nothing to do with men. All signs of **male supremacy** were to be removed. These included male control of employment, politics and the media.

These women believed that even not wearing make-up was an act of protest against male supremacy and were determined to get as much publicity for their cause as possible. For example, they burned their bras, as these were also seen as a symbol of male domination. In 1968, others picketed the Miss America beauty contest in Atlantic City and even crowned a sheep 'Miss America'. The whole contest, they argued, degraded the position of women.

However, the activities of the Women's Liberation Movement did more harm than good. Their extreme actions and protests brought the wrong sort of publicity. Burning their bras in public brought ridicule to the movement and made it increasingly difficult for men and other women to take the whole issue of women's rights seriously. They were a distraction from the key issues of equal pay and better job opportunities.

Achievements of the women's movement

Table 5.1 outlines some of the key achievements of the women's movement from the 1960s to the 1990s.

There has been considerable progress in female employment. Over 70 per cent of women of working age were in employment in 1995 as compared to 38 per cent 40 years earlier. However:

- many of these were in traditional female occupations, such as secretaries and receptionists; only 30 per cent of managers were female
- over two-thirds of part-time jobs were done by women
- average women's earnings were about 75 per cent of those of men in 1998.

Date	Achievement
1963	The Equal Pay Act required employers to pay women the same as men for the same job.
1964	The Civil Rights Act made it illegal to discriminate on the grounds of gender. However, the Equal Opportunities Commission did not take female discrimination seriously, so the Act was not fully enforced in this respect.
1970	In February, about 20 NOW members disrupted the Senate hearings to demand progress on the Equal Rights Amendment (ERA). However, the ERA became bogged down in Congress and was finally defeated in 1982.
1972	The Educational Amendment Act outlawed sex discrimination in education so that girls could follow exactly the same curriculum as boys. This, in turn, would give them greater career opportunities. However, it took a long time for schools to change their traditional curriculum and for the benefits to filter through to the education of girls.
1972	The Supreme Court ruled that the US Constitution did give men and women equal rights.
1973	A feminist lawyer, Sarah Weddington, defended the right of one of her clients, Norma McCorvey, named Jane Roe to protect her anonymity, to have an abortion. In the case *Roe* v. *Wade*, the Supreme Court established a woman's right to abortion, effectively cancelling the anti-abortion laws of 46 states.
1978	The Pregnancy Discrimination Act banned employment discrimination against pregnant women.
1981	Sandra Day O'Connor was the first woman ever appointed to the US Supreme Court. In 1993, she was joined by Ruth Bader Ginsberg.
1983	Dr Sally Ride became the first American woman in space on the shuttle Challenger (STS-7).
1984	Geraldine Ferraro was the first female vice-presidential candidate of a major political party (Democratic Party).
1994	Congress adopted the Gender Equity in Education Act to train teachers in gender equality, promote maths and science learning by girls, counsel pregnant teens, and prevent sexual harassment.

▲ Table 5.1: Achievements of the Women's Liberation Movement, 1963–94

ACTIVITY

List the achievements and limitations of the women's movement in a table. Overall, was it a success? Explain your answer.

Practice question

The lives of many American women during the period from 1945 to 1990 were influenced by developments such as:

- the impact of the Second World War
- the work of the National Organisation for Women (NOW)
- the work of the Women's Liberation Movement.

Arrange these developments in order of their significance in influencing the lives of American women during this period. *(For guidance, see pages 110–11.)*

6 Cold War rivalry

In 1945 the leaders of the USA, Britain and the USSR met at two peace conferences, Yalta and Potsdam, to decide the future of Germany and Eastern Europe. By the end of the second conference at Potsdam, the USA and USSR had become rivals in what became known as the Cold War, which lasted for over 40 years. A hot war is a conflict in which actual fighting takes place. A cold war is a war waged against an enemy by every means short of actually fighting. The USA adopted a policy of containment to stop the spread of communism in Europe and then the wider world. This led to a series of crises between the two superpowers, particularly the Berlin Crisis of 1948–49 and the Cuban Missile Crisis of 1962. In addition, the USA became involved in the conflict in Vietnam in order to prevent a communist takeover of the country. This conflict brought much opposition within the USA, especially from the student movement, and led to the eventual defeat and withdrawal of American troops.

Reasons for US involvement in the Cold War

During the Second World War, out of necessity, the USA and USSR worked together in order to defeat their common enemy, Hitler and Nazi Germany. However, once Hitler's regime was defeated, in May 1945, relations between the two **superpowers** began to deteriorate (Source A).

> **Source A:** Joseph Stalin speaking in 1945 about his allies Churchill, the British prime minister, and Roosevelt, the US president
>
> *Perhaps you think that, because we are allies of the English, we have forgotten who they are and who Churchill is. They find nothing sweeter than to trick their allies. And Churchill? Churchill is the kind who, if you don't watch him, will slip a kopek out of your pocket. And Roosevelt? Roosevelt is not like that. He dips his hand only for bigger coins.*

In the years after 1945 the USA became involved in a cold war with the USSR for several reasons.

Fear of communism

The USA, who believed in **capitalism**, feared the spread of **communism**. This fear originated with the **Bolshevik Revolution** in 1917, especially as the Bolsheviks believed in worldwide revolution to spread communism. This fear was evident in the **Red Scare**, the growing fear of communism in the USA in the years after the Second World War, and McCarthyism, the practice of making accusations of communism led by Senator Joe McCarthy with little or no real evidence, of the late 1940s and 1950s.

Soviet expansion in Eastern Europe

Having freed much of Eastern Europe from the Nazis, the **Red Army** remained in occupation in this area and the **Soviet Union** established communist governments that were closely controlled from Moscow. These became known as Soviet satellite states and included Poland, Romania, Bulgaria, Czechoslovakia and Hungary. Truman was convinced that Stalin wanted to expand into Western Europe.

Attitude of Truman

In April 1945 Harry Truman became President of the USA. Truman distrusted Stalin and was convinced that the USSR intended to take over the whole of Europe. He was determined to stand up to the Soviet leader. On 16 July 1945, America successfully tested an atomic bomb at a desert site in the USA. At the start of the Potsdam Conference, Truman informed Stalin about this. The Soviet leader was furious that he had not been consulted beforehand.

Post-war peace conferences: Yalta and Potsdam

The Yalta Conference of January 1945 was attended by Churchill, Stalin and Roosevelt. Here it was agreed that Germany and Berlin would be divided into four zones. However, there were differences over how much Germany should pay in reparations and over the future government of Poland.

The Potsdam Conference was the second peace conference of 1945. Truman and Stalin had several disagreements. Twenty million Russians had died during the war and Stalin wanted massive compensation that would have totally and permanently crippled Germany. Truman refused. He saw a revived Germany as a possible barrier to future Soviet expansion. Truman wanted free elections in the countries of Eastern Europe occupied by Soviet troops. Stalin refused to submit to US pressure, believing it was unwelcome interference. Truman was furious and began a 'get tough' policy against the USSR.

At the Potsdam Conference, it was agreed:

- to divide Germany and Berlin as previously agreed. Each of the four zones of Germany and four sectors of Berlin was occupied and administered by one of the Allies
- to demilitarise Germany
- to re-establish democracy in Germany including free elections, a free press and freedom of speech
- that Germany had to pay reparations to the Allies in equipment and materials. Most of this would go to the USSR, which had suffered most. The USSR would be given a quarter of the industrial goods made in the western zones in return for food and coal from the Soviet zone
- to ban the Nazi Party. Nazis were removed from important positions and leading Nazis were put on trial for war crimes at Nuremberg in 1946
- to participate fully in the United Nations organisation
- that Poland's frontier was to be moved westwards to the rivers Oder and Neisse.

> **Source B:** Clement Attlee, the British prime minister, recalling the Potsdam Conference in 1960
>
> *The Russians had shown themselves even more difficult than anyone expected. After Potsdam, one couldn't be very hopeful any longer. It was quite obvious they were going to be troublesome. The war had left them holding positions far into Europe, much too far. I had no doubt they intended to use them.*

The Long Telegram

George Kennan was the USA's Deputy Chief Mission at the US Embassy in Moscow in 1946. He saw the USSR as aggressive and suspicious and recommended firm action by the USA against what he viewed as Soviet expansion in Eastern Europe. His telegram, which became known as the Long Telegram, greatly influenced Truman's policies in the Cold War, especially his policy of containment.

> **Source C:** Extract from the Kennan's Long Telegram, February 1946
>
> *It is clear that the United States cannot expect in the foreseeable future to be close to Soviet regime. It must continue to regard the Soviet Union as a rival, not a partner, in the political arena. It must continue to expect that Soviet policies will reflect no abstract love of peace and stability, no real faith in the possibility of a permanent happy coexistence of the communist and capitalist worlds. Rather, Soviet policies will be a cautious, persistent pressure toward the disruption and weakening of all rival influence and rival power.*

ACTIVITIES

1. Read Source A. What is Stalin's view of his allies?
2. What does Source C show you about the attitude of the USA to Soviet expansion into Eastern Europe?
3. Which was the most important reason for US involvement in the Cold War? Give reasons for your decisions.

Practice question

Describe what was agreed by the Allies in the Yalta and Potsdam Conferences. *(For guidance, see page 108.)*

The Truman Doctrine and containment of communism

In March 1946 Winston Churchill made a speech at Fulton, Missouri, USA which showed how divided Europe had become within less than a year of the end of the Second World War. In this very famous speech he suggested that 'From Stettin in the Baltic to Trieste in the Adriatic, an iron curtain has descended across the continent of Europe.'

In 1947 Britain, who had been giving financial aid to Greece and Turkey since 1944, told the USA they could no longer afford to continue. The USA stepped in with the necessary financial aid, fearing that these two countries would come under Soviet influence. Truman announced US support in an important speech in March 1947. The speech marked a turning point in US foreign policy. He was committing the USA to a policy of containment that became known as the Truman Doctrine (Source D).

> **Source D:** The Truman Doctrine, 12 March 1947
>
> *I believe that it must be the policy of the United States to support peoples who resist being enslaved by armed minorities or by outside pressure. I believe that we must help free peoples to work out their own destiny in their own way.*

Consequences of the Truman Doctrine

As a result of the Truman Doctrine:

- the Greek government was able to defeat the communists
- the rivalry between the USA and the USSR increased. Truman had publicly stated that the world was divided between two ways of life: the free, non-communist and the unfree, communist. Within a year the first serious crisis of the Cold War would begin over Berlin
- the USA became committed to the policy of containment and far more involved in European affairs
- the USA decided to provide economic aid to Europe, known as the Marshall Plan (see below)
- in 1947 Stalin set up the Communist Information Bureau, Cominform, to link communist parties in eastern Europe and worldwide, in common action.

Source E: President Truman announcing the Truman Doctrine to Congress in March 1947

The Marshall Plan

Truman backed up his policy of containment with economic aid to Europe. This was known as the Marshall Plan. He believed that communism generally won support in countries where there were economic problems, unemployment and poverty. Many European countries had suffered badly as a result of the Second World War and were struggling to deal with the damage caused. There were shortages of nearly everything, which led countries to implement rationing. If the USA could help these countries to recover economically and provide employment and reasonable prosperity, then there would be no need to turn to communism.

The plan, officially called the European Recovery Plan but nicknamed the Marshall Plan, was announced by the US Secretary of State, General George Marshall, in June 1947. This aid would take the form of cash, machinery, food and technological assistance. In return, these countries would agree to buy US goods and allow US companies to invest capital in their industries.

US machinery helped European factories to recover from the effects of the Second World War. US advisers helped to rebuild transport systems. Europe became more firmly divided between East and West. Stalin was initially involved but withdrew the USSR from discussions because he did not trust the USA and did not want to show how weak the USSR really was economically. He prevented Eastern European countries, such as Czechoslovakia and Poland, from being involved. By 1953 the USA had provided US$17 billion in Marshall Aid.

Domino Theory

Containment was based on the Domino Theory, the belief that if one country fell to communism this would trigger the fall of its neighbouring countries. The theory was later applied to Asia (see page 89).

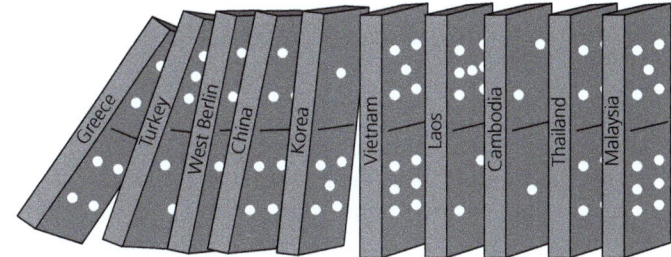

▲ Figure 6.1: The Domino Theory

ACTIVITIES

1. According to Source D what was the aim of the Truman Doctrine?
2. What can you learn from Source F about the Marshall Plan?
3. What does Figure 6.1 show you about the Domino Theory?
4. In less than 10 words summarise the Truman Doctrine, Marshall Plan and the Domino Theory.

Practice question

How far had relations between the USA and the USSR changed between 1945 and 1948? *(For guidance, see page 109.)*

◀ Source F: Berliners using money from the Marshall Plan to help rebuild buildings destroyed during the Second World War

The Berlin crisis 1948–49

Truman put his policy of containment into practice with the Berlin crisis of 1948–49 and the setting up of the North Atlantic Treaty Organisation (NATO) in 1949. The Berlin Blockade was the first major crisis of the Cold War and worsened relations between the superpowers even further.

Reasons for crisis

During the peace conferences of 1945 at Yalta (February) and Potsdam (July), the Allies had agreed to divide both Germany and Berlin into four zones of occupation (Figure 6.2). Berlin was in the heart of Soviet-controlled East Germany and the western Allies were allowed access to their sectors by road, rail, canal and air.

The western Allies forged ahead by encouraging the economic recovery of their zones, especially in providing a much-needed currency. The western zones received large quantities of Marshall Aid (page 83). In addition they set up free elections to establish democracy. This was in sharp contrast with Soviet policies. Stalin feared a strong, democratic and reunited Germany on the borders of the USSR. He feared that a 'western' currency and democratic ideas would spread to the Soviet zone and undermine control of East Berlin. When, in 1948, the Allies announced plans to create a West German state and a new currency, Stalin accused the West of interfering in the Soviet zone.

▲ Figure 6.2: Map showing the division of Germany and Berlin

Events of crisis

On 24 June 1948, Stalin cut off road, rail and canal traffic to Berlin from the western zone of Germany in an attempt to starve the Allies out of West Berlin.

Truman was determined to stand up to the USSR and show that he was serious about containment (see page 82). He saw Berlin as a test case. If the western Allies gave in to Stalin on this issue, the western zones of Germany might be next. Truman wanted Berlin to be a symbol of freedom behind the Iron Curtain.

The only way into Berlin was by air, so the Allies decided to airlift supplies from their bases in West Germany. Would the USSR shoot down these planes? There were anxious moments as the first planes flew over Berlin, but no shots were fired.

The airlift began on 28 June 1948 and lasted for 10 months. The British codenamed it 'Operation Plainfare'. It was the start of the biggest airlift in history. Soon planes were flying day and night along the air corridors. The airlift continued into the spring and reached its peak on 16–17 April 1949 when 1,398 flights landed nearly 13,000 tonnes of supplies in 24 hours. During the airlift West Berliners were supplied with everything from food and clothing to oil and building materials, although there were still great shortages in the city and many decided to leave. During this period there were a total of 275,000 flights with an average of 4,000 tonnes of supplies each day.

Results of crisis

On 12 May 1949 Stalin called off the blockade. He had failed to starve the Allies out of Berlin. That evening Berliners put on evening dress and danced in the streets. The crisis greatly increased East–West rivalry, confirmed the divisions of Germany and Berlin and led to the creation of NATO. Truman saw the outcome of the crisis as a great victory. West Berlin had survived and stood up to the USSR. His policy of containment had worked.

THE BIRD WATCHER

ACTIVITIES

1. What is the message of Source G?
2. Working in pairs, put together contrasting newspaper headlines announcing the end of the airlift (one from a Soviet perspective and one from a US perspective).

Practice question

Explain why the Berlin Crisis of 1948–49 was important in the development of the Cold War. *(For guidance, see page 112.)*

◀ **Source G:** A British cartoon of July 1948. The man holding the gun is Stalin and the storks represent the planes carrying supplies

ACTIVITIES

1. Why was NATO set up?
2. What can you learn from Source H about the aims of NATO?
3. What message is the cartoonist trying to get across in Source I?

Practice question

Describe the Berlin Crisis of 1961. *(For guidance, see page 108.)*

NATO

The Berlin crisis had confirmed Truman's commitment to containment in Europe and highlighted the Soviet threat to Western Europe. The Western European states were aware that, even joined together, they were no match for the USSR and needed the formal support of the USA. In April 1949 the North Atlantic Treaty was signed, establishing NATO. Although a defensive alliance (Source H), its main purpose was to prevent Soviet expansion.

The countries agreed that an armed attack against one or more of them in Europe or North America would be considered an attack against them all. Stalin saw NATO as an 'aggressive alliance' aimed against the USSR. Within six years, in 1955, the USSR had set up its own rival organisation known as the **Warsaw Pact**. It was a military alliance of eight nations headed by the USSR and was designed to counter the threat of NATO. Members were to support each other if attacked. A joint command structure was set up under the Soviet supreme commander. The creation of these two powerful and rival military power blocks exacerbated the tension of the Cold War.

> **Source H:** Extracts from the NATO charter
>
> *Article 3: To achieve the aims of the Treaty, the Parties will keep up their individual and collective capacity to resist armed attack.*
>
> *Article 5: The Parties agree that an armed attack against one or more of them in Europe or North America shall be considered an attack against them all.*

The Berlin crisis, 1961

In the early 1960s Berlin again became a major flashpoint in Cold War relations. In August 1961, Khrushchev, the leader of the USSR, ordered the construction of a wall to separate East Berlin from West Berlin. From January 1961 the number of refugees leaving East Berlin had increased to 20,000 a month. This had to be stopped. Moreover, Khrushchev thought he could bully the new, inexperienced president of the USA, John F. Kennedy. From 5 p.m. on 27 October to 11 a.m. on 28 October, US and Soviet tanks, fully armed, faced each other in a tense stand-off. Then, after 18 hours, the US tanks pulled back. Kennedy had been forced to back down but was furious with the USSR.

▼ **Source I:** A Soviet cartoon showing the NATO generals goose-stepping. This had been the Nazi method of marching. The overall commander in the foreground is carrying a nuclear bomb and a portrait of Hitler

The Cuban Missile Crisis

The Cuban Missile Crisis, which took place over a few days in October 1962, brought the superpowers to the brink of nuclear war. The crisis showed how the Cold War had spread outside the confines of Europe into the wider world.

Causes

The USA had long played an important part in Cuban affairs, propping up the military dictatorship of Batista since 1934. Cuba had become very much a playground for American businessmen. However, Cuba became a thorn in the side of the USA in 1959, when a revolution had brought Fidel Castro to power. Castro had ejected all US businesses and investment. In retaliation, the USA refused to buy Cuba's biggest export – sugar. The USSR offered to buy Cuban sugar. The Soviet leader Khrushchev was keen to extend Soviet influence in the Caribbean and wanted to outmanoeuvre Kennedy.

In April 1961 Kennedy sanctioned an invasion of Cuba by exiles who had left Cuba in 1959. The Bay of Pigs invasion was a disastrous failure due to poor planning and lack of support in Cuba, where Castro was popular. It was a humiliation for the USA; it further strengthened Castro's position in Cuba and drew Cuba even closer to the USSR. At the end of 1961, Castro announced his conversion to communism.

Khrushchev now saw the opportunity to further extend Soviet influence in Cuba. He was concerned by US missile bases in Italy and Turkey and wanted to establish Soviet bases in Cuba to redress the balance. In September 1962, Soviet technicians began to install ballistic missiles on Cuba. On 14 October an American U-2 spy plane took photographs of Cuba which showed that Soviet intermediate-range missile launch sites were being constructed. These could hit almost all US cities and posed a serious threat to the country's security (Figure 6.3).

◀ Figure 6.3: Map showing the USSR's military build-up on Cuba and the range of the nuclear missiles

Events

The crisis lasted 13 days in October 1962 and the events are outlined in Table 6.1.

16 October	Kennedy was told that Khrushchev intended to build missile sites on Cuba.
18–19 October	Kennedy held talks with his closest advisers. The 'Hawks' wanted an aggressive policy whilst the 'Doves' favoured a peaceful solution.
20 October	Kennedy decided to impose a naval blockade around Cuba to prevent Soviet missiles reaching Cuba. US forces searched any ship suspected of carrying arms or missiles.
21 October	Kennedy made a broadcast to the American people, informing them of the potential threat and what he intended to do.
23 October	Khrushchev sent a letter to Kennedy insisting that Soviet ships would force their way through the blockade.
24 October	Khrushchev issued a statement insisting that the USSR would use nuclear weapons in the event of a war.
25 October	Kennedy wrote to Khrushchev asking him to withdraw missiles from Cuba.
26 October	Khrushchev replied to Kennedy's letter. He said he would withdraw the missiles if the USA promised not to invade Cuba and withdrew its missiles from Turkey.
27 October	A US spy plane was shot down over Cuba. Robert Kennedy (brother of the president) agreed a deal with the USSR. The USA would withdraw missiles from Turkey as long as the deal was kept secret.
28 October	Khrushchev accepted the deal.

▲ Table 6.1: Events of the Cuban Missile Crisis

Results

The Cuban crisis had several important effects.

- Kennedy seemed to have won the war of words and the perception was that Khrushchev had backed down, especially as the deal over Turkey was not disclosed at the time.
- The superpowers had played a game of **brinkmanship**. This was typical of the Cold War and means pushing a situation to the verge of war, in order to encourage or threaten your opponent to back down.
- The superpowers had almost gone to war – a war that would have destroyed much of the world. There was a relief that the crisis was over and there was a great reduction in tension. To ensure that the two leaders did not have to communicate by letter in the case of a crisis, a hotline telephone link was established between the White House in Washington DC and the Kremlin in Moscow.
- Further improvements came when the Partial Test Ban Treaty was signed in August 1963 whereby both the USA and the USSR agreed to stop testing nuclear weapons in the atmosphere.
- The case for intervention to turn back communism had been shown to be too dangerous.

ACTIVITIES

1. Working in pairs – one representing the government of the USSR and the other the government of the USA – prepare a speech which clearly supports your actions during the crisis.
2. What were the effects of the Cuban Missile Crisis on each of the following?
   - ☐ Superpower relations
   - ☐ The world
   - ☐ Cuba
   - ☐ The USSR
   - ☐ The USA.

Practice question

Explain why the Cuban Missile Crisis was important in the history of the Cold War. *(For guidance, see page 112.)*

6 Cold War rivalry

US involvement in Vietnam

Under President Johnson the USA became directly involved in the war in Vietnam. This involvement was to have major effects on US foreign and domestic policy.

Reasons for US involvement

Vietnam had been a French colony, but the defeat of the French in 1954 resulted in far greater US involvement. This was part of the US policy of containment in order to stop the spread of communism. The fundamental reason was the Domino Theory (see page 83). The USA was convinced that if Vietnam fell to communism it would be followed by its neighbouring states, especially Laos and Cambodia. US involvement increased in the years 1954–64 as Table 6.2 shows.

ACTIVITY

Make a copy of the table below showing possible reasons for US involvement in Vietnam in the 1950s and 1960s. Give each reason a rating of 1–5 for their importance (from 1 = unimportant to 5 = decisive). Give a brief explanation for each decision.

Reasons	Ratings
Contain communism	
Defend democracy	
Extend US influence	

▲ Figure 6.4: Map showing the division of Vietnam in 1954

Practice question

Explain why the USA became more involved in Vietnam in the years 1954–64. *(For guidance, see page 112.)*

Date	Reason	US policy
1954	The Geneva Agreement	This followed the defeat of the French at Dien Bien Phu by the **Vietminh**. Vietnam would be divided temporarily along the 17th parallel into North and South Vietnam (Figure 6.4). North Vietnam would be led by Ho Chi Minh (communist) and the South would be led by Ngo Dinh Diem (non-communist). The USA prevented early elections for a new government in July 1956, realising that the communists would win.
1959	**Vietcong** terror campaign	Ho Chi Minh issued orders to the Vietminh (who became known as the Vietcong) to begin a terror campaign against the South.
1963	Overthrow of Diem	In November 1963 Diem, who was a corrupt and unpopular ruler, was overthrown and replaced by a series of short-lived and weak governments. The Vietcong became more popular in the South.
1963	Failure of 'Strategic Hamlet Policy'	Under Kennedy, the USA tried to reduce communist influence through this policy. It involved moving Vietnamese peasants into fortified villages, guarded by troops. It did not stop the communists and was very unpopular with Vietnamese peasants.
1964	Gulf of Tonkin incident	President Johnson wanted more direct military involvement in Vietnam but needed an excuse. On 2 August 1964 the US destroyer *Maddox* was fired on by North Vietnamese patrol boats in the Gulf of Tonkin. Johnson was able to use these attacks to persuade Congress to support greater US involvement.

▲ Table 6.2: Events behind increasing US involvement in Vietnam, 1954–64

US methods of warfare in Vietnam

The methods used by the USA in the Vietnam War changed during the course of the 1960s.

'Operation Rolling Thunder'

This was the US bombing campaign of North Vietnam that lasted 3.5 years, from 1965–68, in the hope of destroying Vietcong supply routes to the South. It encouraged even greater support for the war from North Vietnam and did not stop the supplies to the Vietcong from the North.

Chemical warfare

Chemical weapons such as **defoliants** were used to destroy the jungle cover for the Vietcong.

- One such weapon was known as 'Agent Orange', a highly toxic weedkiller used to destroy the jungle. The Americans used 82 million litres of Agent Orange to spray thousands of kilometres of jungle.
- Napalm was another chemical weapon widely used by the USA. It was a type of bomb that exploded and showered the surrounding victims with a burning petroleum jelly. Napalm sticks to the skin and burns at 800°C. It could burn through skin and flesh to the bone.

'Search and destroy'

The US commander in Vietnam, Westmoreland, established secure and heavily defended US bases in the south of the country near the coasts. From here, US and South Vietnamese (ARVN) forces launched 'search and destroy' tactics using helicopters. They would descend on a village suspected of assisting the Vietcong forces and destroy it (Sources J and K). The troops called these attacks 'Zippo' raids after the name of the lighters they used to set fire to the thatched houses of the villages.

- These raids would usually kill a handful of Vietcong guerrilla fighters, but inexperienced US troops often walked into traps.
- Inadequate information often meant that innocent villages were destroyed.
- Civilian casualties were often very high, with most having little or no connection with the Vietcong.
- This, in turn, made the USA and ARVN very unpopular with many South Vietnamese peasants who were then more likely to support the Vietcong.

Source J: An account from Doug Ramsey, a US civilian who was working for the Agency for International Development (AID) in Vietnam. He describes what happened to one village

The rubble of the hamlet was still smoking, and it was obvious that these people had returned only a short time before to discover what had happened to their homes. Children were whimpering. Women were poking through the smouldering debris of the houses trying to save cooking utensils and other small possessions that might have escaped the flames. The soldiers had even burned all of the rice that had not been buried or hidden elsewhere. A middle-aged farmer in the group asked Ramsey what agency he worked for. 'AID', Ramsey replied. 'AID', the farmer cried. 'Look about you', he said whilst pointing at the charred ruins of the village. 'Here is your American AID'! The farmer spat on the ground and walked away.

ACTIVITY

What can you learn from Sources J and K about US search and destroy tactics?

◄ **Source K:** US soldiers destroying a village suspected of supporting the Vietcong

Reasons for US defeat

The USA were eventually defeated in Vietnam through a combination of the strengths of the communists and their own weaknesses (see Table 6.3).

The strengths of the communists	The weaknesses of the USA
Fighting for a cause • The North Vietnamese and Vietcong were fighting for a cause – communism and the reunification of Vietnam. • They refused to surrender even after US bomb attacks. • They were prepared to accept heavy casualties. **Effective guerrilla tactics** • The Vietcong fought a 'low-tech' war using very successful guerrilla tactics which, for the most part, avoided pitched battles and reduced the effectiveness of the 'high-tech' methods and superior weaponry of the USA (Source L). • These methods were ideally suited to the jungle terrain of South Vietnam. **Support from the USSR and China** • Both of these countries supported the reunification of Vietnam under the communist North. They supplied the North and Vietcong with rockets, tanks and fighter planes. **Support from the South Vietnamese** Many in the South supported the North and the Vietcong: • Some believed in communism and reunification. Others were alienated by US tactics and brutality. • Their support, in turn, made the Vietcong guerrilla tactics far more effective. **The tunnels** The communist forces dug deep tunnels and used them as air-raid shelters. They were also a safe haven for the guerrilla fighters. They often acted as death traps for US and ARVN forces.	**The US troops** • Many were too young and inexperienced and unable to cope with guerrilla warfare (Source M). Most did not understand why they were fighting in Vietnam. • This, in turn, led to a fall in morale with some resorting to drug-taking and brutal behaviour such as that seen in the My Lai massacre where, in March 1968, US troops murdered 347 men, women and children. **Opposition at home** Undermined the war effort and was due to: • a failure to achieve a quick victory • many casualties, with a total of 58,000 deaths • televised pictures showing the horrors of war such as the use of napalm. **Failure of US tactics** • The US army failed to develop an effective response to Vietcong guerrilla tactics. • US tactics, especially 'search and destroy' and chemical warfare, encouraged even greater Vietnamese peasant support for the Vietcong in the countryside. **The Tet Offensive** On 31 January 1968, the Vietcong launched a massive attack on over 100 cities and towns in South Vietnam during the New Year, or Tet holiday. This proved an important turning point in the conflict: • It showed that the Vietcong could strike at the heart of the American-held territory. Even the US Embassy in Saigon was captured. • It brought a further loss of US military morale. • To the US public, the war seemed unwinnable and it fuelled further criticism of US involvement.

▲ Table 6.3: Reasons for US defeat in Vietnam

▲ **Source L:** A Vietnamese poster of 1968 showing the guerrilla warfare used by the Vietcong

> **Source M:** A US soldier remembers his first battle. From C. Culpin, *Making History*, 1996
>
> *We were in the middle of dense jungle with insects everywhere. Oh God, I was so scared! My stomach was churning. I suspected I was going to vomit and also have a bowel movement at the same time. I remember thinking I would rather throw up because it would not show. The last thing I wanted to do was fight.*

ACTIVITIES

1. Produce a mind map showing the reasons for US defeat in Vietnam. Draw lines to show links between the reasons, giving a brief explanation for the link along each line.
2. What do Source L and M suggest about the conditions facing US soldiers in Vietnam?

The US withdrawal and peace talks

By 1969, more than 36,000 members of the US military had been killed in the war. In May of that year, President Nixon, who had been elected the previous year on a promise of withdrawing US troops from Vietnam, unveiled his plan to end US involvement, known as Vietnamisation. The idea was that the South Vietnamese soldiers would be trained and equipped to take the place of US troops as they were gradually withdrawn. The strategy did not work because the South Vietnamese troops were no match for the communist forces.

Peace talks to end the war had begun as early as 1968 but, for the next four years, there was no real progress as each side haggled over minor issues, such as the shape and size of the meeting table, where people would sit, who would be in meetings, whether or not they would have small flags on the table, and other petty issues. One major issue confronting the negotiators was the inclusion of the South Vietnamese communists as a separate negotiating group. South Vietnamese President Thieu did not want them at any meetings because he knew this gave the Vietcong legal status. The Vietcong had no form of government, no recognised leader and had disrupted life in South Vietnam. Nonetheless, they were granted an official position at the table.

The turning point came with Nixon's visit to China in 1972 after which the Chinese encouraged more co-operation from the government of North Vietnam. On 23 January 1973, a ceasefire was signed in Paris (Source N), followed four days later by a formal peace treaty in which the USA promised to withdraw fully all its troops and the Vietcong was allowed to hold on to all captured areas of South Vietnam. Within two years, the communists had defeated the South Vietnamese armed forces and reunited Vietnam. The US had failed in its attempts to stop the spread of communism in south-east Asia. Cambodia and Laos also fell to communism, proving the Domino Theory partially true.

ACTIVITIES

1. What was the significance of Nixon's Vietnamisation policy?
2. Why did the involvement of the USA in Vietnam end?

▼ **Source N:** Le Duc Tho (right), leader of the North Vietnam delegation in Paris, and Henry Kissinger (left) at the Paris peace talks, November 1972

The effects of the war

- US involvement in the war was very expensive. In 1964 the war cost the taxpayer under half a billion dollars but, within four years, this had increased to US$26.5 billion dollars. The war was the main contributor to the government's US$26 billion deficit and to rising inflation in 1968. The huge annual spending on the war did much to undermine Johnson's spending on the Great Society (see page 56).
- The war made President Johnson very unpopular and heavily influenced his decision not to seek re-election as president in 1968.
- The Treasury warning that the war could not go on, together with taxpayer resentment, helped to convince Johnson that the escalation of the war must stop and Nixon that the war must end.
- The American policy of containment had failed. The war had shown that even the USA's vast military strength could not stop the spread of communism. Not only did the USA fail to stop Vietnam becoming communist, but the heavy bombing of Vietnam's neighbours, Laos and Cambodia, encouraged support for communism in both countries. Indeed, by 1975, Laos and Cambodia had communist governments. Far from slowing down the domino effect, US policies had advanced the process in south-east Asia.
- The Vietnam War was also a propaganda disaster for the USA and did much to lessen its influence in world affairs. It was shown to be propping up a corrupt government in South Vietnam. Moreover, the atrocities committed by American soldiers and the use of chemical weapons damaged the reputation of the USA and its defence of capitalism.
- The inability to win the war pushed Nixon into considering different diplomatic strategies that affected the Cold War. His decision to visit China to establish closer relations, and also to develop détente (see page 94) with the USSR, were attempts to drive a wedge between the two main supporters of North Vietnam.
- From the war emerged the Nixon Doctrine which stated that the USA expected its allies to take care of their own military defence. The Vietnam War was the first war that the USA had lost and there was an unwillingness to become involved in future conflicts.

ACTIVITY

Using a mind map summarise the main effects of the war on the USA.

▲ Source O: Bronze sculpture erected in Washington DC, in honour of those who fought in the Vietnam War

7 The search for world peace since 1970

During the 1970s the USA supported a policy of improved relations with the USSR, known as détente. The key features of this policy were the Helsinki Agreements and Nixon's visit to China. This warming of friendship came to an abrupt end with the Soviet invasion of Afghanistan in 1979, which plunged the world into a second phase of the Cold War. However, during the late 1980s co-operation between the USA and USSR improved once again due to the close working relationship of Reagan and Gorbachev and was followed by the end of the Cold War. The last 20 years of the twentieth century, on the other hand, saw the USA become increasingly concerned about developments in the Middle East, especially in Iran and Iraq.

Détente and attempts to limit arms

The improvement in relations between the USA and the USSR in the years after the Cuban Missile Crisis (see pages 87–88) became known as détente – a French word that means a reduction in tension.

Reasons for détente

This relaxation in relations was due to several reasons.

- The threat of a nuclear war during the Cuban Missile Crisis had had a sobering effect on all concerned. The hotline between the White House and the Kremlin improved the speed of communications and the Test Ban Treaty (see page 88) showed a willingness to look at the issue of developing nuclear missiles.
- Both the USA and the USSR were keen on arms limitation talks as a means of reducing their ever-increasing defence spending.
- The USA involvement in Vietnam had not gone well and, by 1968, the USA was seeking to end the war. After Nixon became president it was hoped that if the USA improved trade and technology links and made an offer of arms reduction, then Leonid Brezhnev, the Soviet leader, might persuade his North Vietnamese ally to negotiate an end to the war. The idea of offering concessions was called '**linkage**' by Nixon's advisers. Nixon visited Moscow in 1972 and made it clear that he did not see Vietnam as an obstacle to détente.
- Nixon had visited China three months earlier (see page 96) and Brezhnev did not want to see a Chinese–US alliance develop. The Soviet leader was keen to gain access to US technology and further grain sales.
- The Soviet invasion of Czechoslovakia in 1968 gave rise to the Brezhnev Doctrine. This declared that all member countries had to remain part of the **Warsaw Pact**. In other words, the USSR would put down any attempt to suppress communist control. This alarmed the USA and showed the need for dialogue between the two **superpowers**.

> **ACTIVITIES**
>
> 1 Make a Venn diagram showing the reasons for détente.
> 2 Using a mind map, summarise the main features of détente.
> 3 What information does Source A provide about relations between the USA and the USSR in the early 1970s?

Détente in action

The most significant features of détente were the SALT agreements and the Helsinki Agreements.

The SALT agreements

SALT stands for Strategic Arms Limitation Treaty. There were two such treaties. The main features of the SALT I and SALT II are outlined in Table 7.1 below.

The Helsinki Agreements, 1975

In July 1974 Nixon visited Moscow. After the meeting the two leaders agreed to develop broad, mutually beneficial co-operation in commercial, economic, scientific, technical and cultural fields. The aim was to promote increased understanding and confidence between the peoples of both countries. The Helsinki Agreements of 1975 were a product of this. The USA and the USSR, along with 33 other nations, made declarations about three distinct international issues (called 'baskets' by the signatories (Figure 7.1)).

▲ **Source A:** Brezhnev (left) and Nixon (right) at the signing of SALT I in 1972

	SALT I	SALT II

Terms	• Early in Nixon's presidency, a decision was made to talk about nuclear weapons. Talks held in Helsinki and Vienna over a period of almost three years produced SALT I, the first Strategic Arms Limitation Treaty, which imposed limits on the nuclear capability of the USSR and the USA.
	• The two superpowers agreed that there would be no further production of strategic ballistic missiles (short-range, lightweight missiles). Both powers agreed that submarines carrying nuclear weapons would only be introduced when existing stocks of intercontinental ballistic missiles (ICBM) became obsolete.
		• Final agreements for SALT II were reached in June 1979. The terms were:
		  • a limit of 2,400 strategic nuclear delivery vehicles for each side
		  • a 1,320 limit on multiple independently targetable re-entry vehicle (MIRV) systems for each side
		  • a ban on the construction of new land-based intercontinental ballistic missiles (ICBM) launchers.
		• The agreement would last until 1985.

Significance	SALT I was significant because it was the first agreement between the superpowers that successfully limited the number of nuclear weapons they held.	The US Senate refused to ratify the SALT II agreements following the Soviet invasion of Afghanistan, December 1979.

▲ Table 7.1: A summary of the SALT agreements

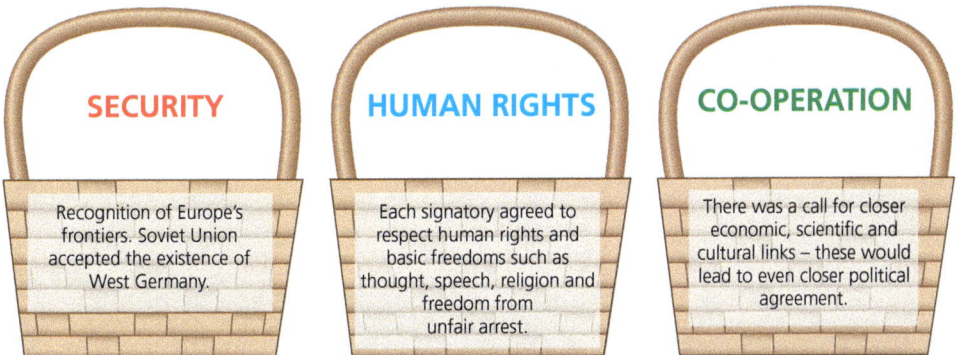

SECURITY — Recognition of Europe's frontiers. Soviet Union accepted the existence of West Germany.

HUMAN RIGHTS — Each signatory agreed to respect human rights and basic freedoms such as thought, speech, religion and freedom from unfair arrest.

CO-OPERATION — There was a call for closer economic, scientific and cultural links – these would lead to even closer political agreement.

▲ Figure 7.1: The three issues (or 'baskets') discussed under the Helsinki Agreements, 1975

Practice questions

1. Describe the Helsinki Agreements. *(For guidance, see page 108.)*
2. Explain why relations between the USA and the USSR changed during the 1970s. *(For guidance, see page 112.)*

Changing relations with China

In October 1970, in an interview with *Time* magazine, Nixon said: 'If there is anything I want to do before I die, it is to go to China.' In the early 1970s, he was to achieve this wish.

Reasons

There were several reasons for improved relations between the USA and China.

- Relations between China and the USSR had worsened in the later 1960s, especially after the Chinese denounced the Soviet invasion of Czechoslovakia in 1968. Nixon saw an opportunity to exploit this split between the two leading communist nations.
- Nixon also hoped that closer relations with China might help to end the war in Vietnam, as the Chinese were close allies of the North Vietnamese (see page 91). This was another example of his policy of linkage.

Ping-pong diplomacy

'Ping-pong diplomacy' began at the World Table Tennis Championship held in Japan on 6 April 1971, when the Chinese ping-pong team formally invited the US team to play in their country on an all-expenses paid trip. When American player Glenn Cowan missed his team's bus after practice, he was offered a ride by Chinese player, Zhuang Zedong. This friendly display of good will was well publicised and later that day the American team was formally invited to China. They were among the first group of US citizens permitted to visit China since 1949 (Source B).

On 14 April 1971, the US government lifted a trade embargo with China that had lasted over 20 years. Talks began to facilitate a meeting between top government officials and, eventually, a meeting between China's leader Mao Zedong and President Richard Nixon. In February 1972, Nixon would become the first American president to visit China. The meeting did help to normalise relations between the two countries and reduce tensions over Vietnam.

This 'ping-pong diplomacy' was important because it led to the restoration of Sino–US relations which had been cut for more than two decades. This triggered a series of other events, including the restoration of China's legitimate rights in the United Nations by an overwhelming majority vote in October 1971 and the establishment of diplomatic relations between China and other countries. Moreover, the lifting of the embargo with China meant that trade between the two countries could be restored. However, the economic benefits of this were slow as it would take decades for American products to penetrate the vast Chinese market.

ACTIVITY

Study Source B. Why do you think this photograph was publicised?

Practice question

Explain why relations between the USA and China changed during the 1970s. *(For guidance, see page 112.)*

Source B: The US table tennis team pose for a portrait with their guides in front of a pagoda at the Summer Palace near Beijing, China in April 1971

Changing US relations with the USSR

The Soviet invasion of Afghanistan in 1979 brought about a significant worsening of relations between the USA and the USSR which continued until Gorbachev became Soviet leader in the mid-1980s.

Soviet involvement in Afghanistan

On 27 April 1978, the People's Democratic Party of Afghanistan (PDPA), a communist party, overthrew the government of Afghanistan. Nur Muhammad Taraki, Secretary General of the PDPA, became President of the Revolutionary Council and Prime Minister of the newly established Democratic Republic of Afghanistan. During its first 18 months of rule, the PDPA imposed a communist-style reform programme. In addition, thousands of members of the traditional élite – the Muslim religious establishment and intellectuals – were imprisoned, tortured or murdered. In September 1979, Hafizullah Amin, the Deputy Prime Minister, seized power from Taraki, but there was continued instability in the country because of the anti-Muslim policies. Thousands of Afghan Muslims joined the *mujahideen* – a guerrilla movement which proclaimed to be on a holy mission for Allah. They wanted to overthrow the Amin government. The *mujahideen* declared a *jihad* – a holy war – on the supporters of Amin. Brezhnev was concerned about the growing power and spread of Islamic fundamentalism and wanted to show the 30 million Muslims in the USSR that there would be no changes to the way the USSR was run. The USSR saw fundamentalism as a great threat to the Soviet system.

Between 25 December 1979 and 1 January 1980, more than 50,000 Soviet troops were sent to Afghanistan to restore order and protect the PDPA from the *mujahideen*. The invasion was to profoundly change the Cold War and relations between the superpowers.

▲ **Source C:** Soviet troops and tanks in Afghanistan in 1980

The reaction of President Carter

The USA saw that a Soviet-occupied Afghanistan would threaten India and Pakistan and would be a stepping-stone to possible Soviet control of much of the West's oil supplies (Figure 7.2).

President Carter adopted a firm approach with the USSR over the invasion. This was because he was already under pressure in November 1979 following the seizure of US embassy staff as hostages in Iran (see pages 104–5). He had failed to solve that problem by the end of the year, and some in the USA were accusing him of being a weak leader. In addition, he believed it would improve relations with China, who also opposed the invasion (Source C). He therefore adopted a firm approach with the USSR (Source E).

- The Carter Doctrine stated that the USA would use military force if necessary to defend its national interests in the Persian Gulf region. It also promised US military aid to all the countries bordering Afghanistan.
- The tough line was continued when Carter asked the Senate to delay passing the SALT II treaty (see pages 94–5).
- The USA cancelled all shipments of grain to the USSR, and US companies were forbidden to sell high-tech goods there, such as computers and oil drilling equipment.
- Carter pressured the United States Olympic Committee to boycott the 1980 Moscow Olympic Games. Sixty-one other countries followed Carter's example.

> **Source D:** From a newspaper article in the Chinese newspaper, *Beijing People's Daily*, 1 January 1980. It was discussing the Soviet invasion of Afghanistan
>
> The invasion is a stepping-stone for a southward thrust towards Pakistan and India. There will be no peace in Southern Asia with Soviet soldiers in strategic Afghanistan.

> **Source E:** From Carter's State of the Union speech (an annual address by the president to the country) on 23 January 1980
>
> Let our position be absolutely clear: an attempt by any outside force to gain control of the Persian Gulf region will be regarded as an assault on the vital interests of the USA, and such an assault will be repelled by any means necessary, including military force.

ACTIVITY

Study Source D. What can you learn about the reaction of China to the Soviet invasion?

Practice question

Explain why Presidents Carter and Reagan adopted a hardline policy towards the USSR. *(For guidance, see page 112.)*

◀ Figure 7.2: Map showing the geographical importance of Afghanistan

7 The search for world peace since 1970

Reagan and the 'Second Cold War'

Ronald Reagan, who defeated Carter in the 1980 presidential election, believed in taking a far tougher line with the USSR than Carter. He made it clear that he had no interest in détente and was prepared to confront the USSR whenever possible. In a speech to the British House of Commons on 8 June 1982, Reagan called the USSR 'an evil empire'. He was determined to win the Cold War and believed that the USSR could be forced to disarm by his new initiative: SDI (Strategic Defence Initiative).

Strategic Defence Initiative

The Strategic Defence Initiative (SDI), which became known as 'Star Wars' (after the film), took the nuclear arms race to a new level. It proposed a 'nuclear umbrella', which would stop Soviet nuclear bombs from reaching American soil. Reagan's plan was to launch an army of satellites equipped with powerful lasers, which would intercept Soviet missiles in space and destroy them before they could do any harm to the USA (Figure 7.3). He believed that 'Star Wars' technology would make Soviet nuclear missiles useless and force the USSR to disarm.

SDI proved to be a turning point in the arms race. During détente, the superpowers had been evenly matched and had worked together to limit the growth of nuclear stockpiles. SDI was a complete break from this policy. Soviet leaders knew that they could not compete with Reagan's 'Star Wars' plan. They were behind the USA in space and computer technology, while the Soviet economy was not producing enough wealth to fund further defence spending.

By the early 1980s relations between the two superpowers had deteriorated to such an extent that this period is often described as the beginning of the Second Cold War.

Source F: From President Reagan's first press conference at the White House, 31 January 1981

So far, détente has been a one-way street which the USSR has used to pursue its own aims. I know of no leader of the USSR who has not more than once repeated in communist congresses that their goal must be the promotion of world revolution and a one-world communist state.

Source G: Two comments about the Cold War and communism that President Reagan made during his first presidency

Here's my strategy on the Cold War: We win, they lose.

Communism works only in heaven, where they don't need it, and in hell, where they've already got it.

ACTIVITY

Use Sources F and G and your own knowledge to explain President Reagan's attitude towards communism and the USSR.

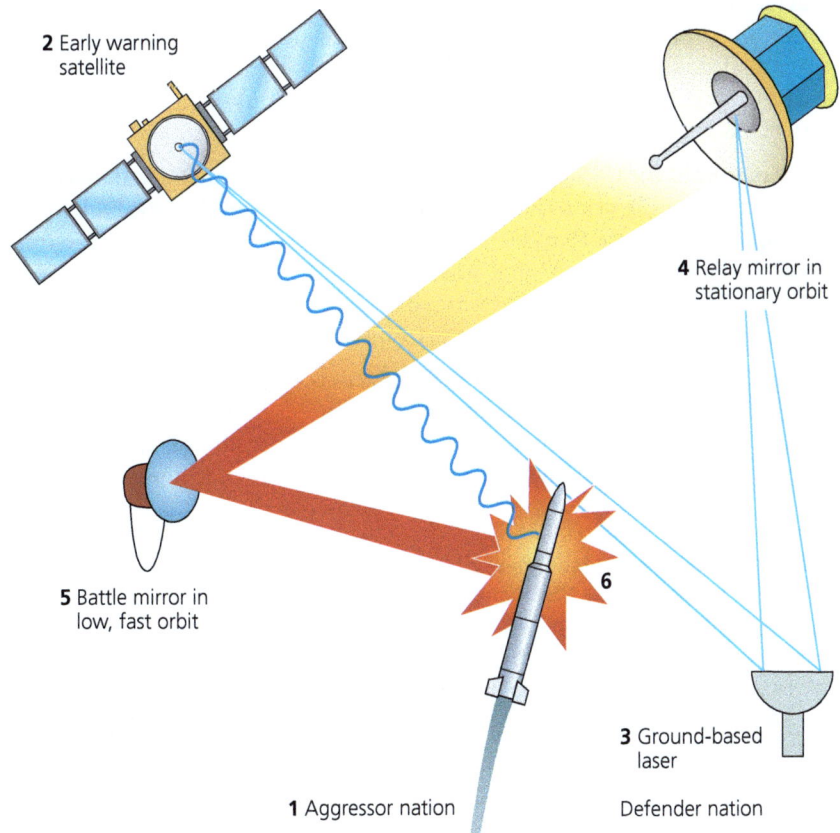

◀ Figure 7.3: The star wars programme

Change under Reagan and Gorbachev

The relationship between the USA and the USSR changed again in the mid-1980s because of Gorbachev's new policies and his relationship with Reagan.

Gorbachev's new policies

Mikhail Gorbachev was the last leader of the USSR, serving as General Secretary from 1985 until its collapse in 1991. He oversaw the end of the Cold War, the fall of the **Berlin Wall** and the end of communism in the USSR. Gorbachev recognised that communism in the USSR faced many problems. For example, the economy was not nearly as efficient as the American economy. While most American people in the 1980s enjoyed a high standard of living, everyday life in the USSR was dominated by shortages. This, in turn, meant that many Soviet people had lost faith in communism.

Gorbachev introduced three important strategies which greatly changed relationships with the West, and more especially the USA.

- He initiated sweeping reforms in the Communist Party and Soviet system in the USSR. These included *perestroika* (restructuring) which meant economic reforms designed to make the Soviet economy more efficient, and *glasnost* (openness) in which censorship of the press was relaxed.
- He ended the arms race with the USA and signed various arms reduction agreements.
- He stopped Soviet interference in eastern European satellite states such as Poland and Czechoslovakia.

At first Reagan reacted in a negative way towards Gorbachev's reforms. He actually made Gorbachev's reforms much more difficult by doing things like giving speeches demanding the general secretary 'tear down this wall'. However, eventually Reagan supported the reforms but refused to 'reward' Gorbachev with economic concessions, believing these might encourage the USSR to revive.

Gorbachev wanted to maintain the USSR's role of superpower. He knew that he had to win over the Soviet people and show the world that he would not threaten world peace. He had to be all things to all people. He assumed that *perestroika* and *glasnost* would strengthen the power of the Soviet Communist Party. However, *glasnost* was a two-edged sword for Gorbachev. The more freedom that people gained, the more they wanted and the more they began to criticise Gorbachev – making it more difficult to maintain the Communist Party's grip on power.

The economy had been damaged by the arms race, the space race, the war in Afghanistan and, above all else, by a system that did not encourage incentive. *Perestroika* did bring some considerable changes and certain aspects of a free economy were introduced. However, these were not fast enough to satisfy many Soviet people or make much difference to their standard of living.

> **Source H:** From an article in *The Sunday Times*, 27 December 1987. The article was discussing Gorbachev's impact on the USSR and the world
>
> *The Soviet Union is different thanks to Gorbachev. In the world beyond the Soviet Union he has been the prime instigator of change. At home the changes are remarkable. Compared with just one year ago, Soviet citizens can now think more freely without fear of reprisal. They can emigrate in increasing numbers. Seeing and reading certain plays, films and novels which were once banned is now no longer considered dangerous. Nevertheless, some foreign stations are still jammed and there are still political prisoners.*

ACTIVITIES

1. What was meant by the following?
   - ☐ Perestroika
   - ☐ Glasnost.
2. What can you learn from Source H about the impact of Gorbachev's policies?

The end of the arms race

Arms limitation talks were renewed after it was clear that Gorbachev was keen to change relations with the West. A summit meeting between Gorbachev and Reagan was held in Geneva over 2 days in November 1985. Though nothing was decided, the Geneva Accord was set out which committed the two countries to speed up arms talks. Both leaders promised to meet in the near future and it was clear to many observers that the two men had got on well.

Intermediate Nuclear Forces Treaty, 1987

Although a second summit meeting at Reykjavik in 1986 failed to reach agreement on arms limitation, a third summit in Washington in December 1987 was more successful, with the signing of the Intermediate Nuclear Forces (INF) Treaty. This treaty eliminated nuclear and conventional ground-launched ballistic and cruise missiles with ranges of 500–5,500 km (300–3,400 miles). By the treaty's deadline, 1 June 1991, a total of 2,692 such weapons had been destroyed; 846 by the USA and 1,846 by the USSR. Also under the treaty, both nations were allowed to inspect each other's military installations.

The INF Treaty was important because it was the first treaty to reduce the number of nuclear missiles that the superpowers possessed. It therefore went much further than SALT I, which simply limited the growth of Soviet and American stockpiles.

Moscow summit

After the signing of the INF Treaty, the final summit meeting was held in Moscow in May 1988. Much of the West seemed to be overtaken by what became known as 'Gorbymania'. It was as if Gorbachev had become a pop star. Furthermore, it was evident that the wives of Gorbachev and Reagan had played a part in pushing the two leaders together.

At the Moscow summit there were more arms control talks. The summit led to the Conventional Forces in Europe (CFE) Treaty, which was signed by NATO and Warsaw Pact representatives in November 1990. The agreement reduced the number of tanks, missiles and aircraft held by the signatory states.

Gorbachev and Bush

The USA and the USSR continued to enjoy good relations. The new US President, George Bush Sr, and Gorbachev were able to announce that the Cold War was over in a summit in Malta in 1989. When Saddam Hussein invaded Kuwait in 1990 (see page 106) the two superpowers acted closely and followed the directives of the United Nations. However, Gorbachev did not commit any troops to the coalition forces that invaded Iraq.

At the Washington summit of 31 May–3 June 1990, Bush and Gorbachev discussed Strategic Arms Limitation (START) and finally signed the Treaty for the Reduction and Limitation of Strategic Arms (START 1), on 31 July 1991. It called for both sides to reduce their strategic nuclear arms over the next seven years. This meant reducing 25 to 35 per cent of all their strategic warheads. Bush and Gorbachev signed the treaty with pens made of scrapped missiles.

> **ACTIVITY**
>
> Put together a timeline to show the key developments in relations between the USA and the USSR in the years 1985–90. You should include on your timeline the summit meetings and arms agreements. Place positive developments above the line and negative developments below. Explain why each was positive or negative.

> **Practice question**
>
> How important was the relationship between Reagan and Gorbachev in bringing about an end to the Cold War? *(For guidance, see page 113–14.)*

◀ Source I: President Reagan (centre) and General Secretary Gorbachev (left) signing the INF Treaty at the White House on 8 December 1987

The fall of Communism and the end of the Cold War

At the Malta Conference in 1989, US President George Bush Snr declared that the Cold War was over. However, it was not until 1991, with the end of communist control of Eastern Europe and the fall of the USSR, that the rivalry between the superpowers really ended.

Changes in Eastern Europe

In December 1988, Gorbachev withdrew Soviet troops from Eastern European bases to save money. In the following year he announced what became known as the Sinatra Doctrine – that members of the Warsaw Pact could make changes to their countries without expecting outside interference. He hoped to strengthen communism in Eastern Europe but all he did was weaken it. Once reform had started in these countries, he was unable to contain it. Figure 7.4 gives an overview of these events in eastern Europe between 1989 and 1991.

▲ Figure 7.4: A map showing the break-up of the Soviet Empire in the years 1988–91

The fall of the Berlin Wall

This event has come to symbolise the end of the Cold War. However, it would be wrong to confuse the fall of the wall with the end of the war. On 9 November 1989, the East German government announced the opening of the border crossings into West Germany. The people began to dismantle the Berlin Wall. Within a few days, over 1 million people had seized the chance to see relatives and experience life in West Germany. West and East Germany were formally reunited in October 1990.

Tension in the world seemed to ease by the day, while the power of the USSR seemed to be dwindling so quickly. The new Germany joined NATO and, in 1991, the Warsaw Pact was dissolved.

The collapse of the USSR

Events in Eastern Europe had a catastrophic impact on the USSR. The many nationalities and ethnic groups saw how the satellite states had been able to break away from Moscow. In 1990, the Baltic states of Estonia, Latvia and Lithuania declared themselves independent, which was accepted by Moscow in 1991. This led to other demands for independence within the USSR.

Gorbachev found that he was opposed by most sections of Soviet society. In August 1991, there was an attempted coup d'etat which was defeated by Boris Yeltsin who was President of the Russian Socialist Republic. Gorbachev was restored as General Secretary but he had lost his authority. Gorbachev resigned in December 1991 and the USSR split into several independent states (Figure 7.5). The fall of the USSR finally ended the rivalry between communism in the East and capitalism in the West. Now there was only one superpower left – the USA.

▲ Figure 7.5: The break-up of the USSR into the Commonwealth of Independent States

ACTIVITIES

1. Construct a flow chart to show how the USSR fell apart (begin and end as follows):

   Rejection of Brezhnev doctrine → ☐ → ☐ → ☐ → ☐ → Collapse of Warsaw Pact

2. Why was the fall of the Berlin Wall so significant?
3. Working in pairs, make a copy of and complete the following table showing whether relations between the USA and the USSR improved or worsened in the years 1970–91. Give a brief explanation for each choice.

Event	Improved	Worsened
SALT 1		
Helsinki Agreements		
Soviet invasion of Afghanistan		Infuriated Carter and led to the Carter Doctrine
SDI		
Gorbachev's new policies		
INF Treaty		

US involvement in Iran, Iraq and the Gulf War

The USA became increasingly involved in the Middle East in the last quarter of the twentieth century, most especially in Iran and Iraq.

Iran

America's closest ally in the Persian Gulf region was Mohammad Reza Pahlavi, the Shah of Iran. For 25 years the Shah had tried to modernise Iran by rapid industrialisation and the emancipation of women. However, this modernisation and his increasingly tyrannical government led to his forced abdication in January 1979. This unsettled the whole region.

- The USA had vital oil interests in the Gulf area and especially Iran (Figure 7.6).
- This period saw the growth of religious fundamentalism in the region which demanded an end to Western (more especially American) imperialism and seriously threatened US Middle Eastern oil interests.
- Iran was now controlled by the fundamentalist religious leader Ayatollah Ruhollah Khomeini, who denounced the USA as the 'Great Satan' and announced an Islamic republic determined to destroy all western influences.

The Iranian hostages

On 4 November 1979, the US Embassy in Tehran was taken over by militant Iranian students (Sources J and K). Sixty-six Americans, including diplomats and their guards, were taken hostage. In return for the release of the hostages, the Ayatollah Khomeini demanded that the USA agree to the extradition of the former Shah who was undergoing medical treatment in New York. The crisis dragged on for over a year:

- The US government refused to hand over the Shah and suspended Iranian oil imports. Carter threatened Iran with military action if the hostages were not released.
- The Ayatollah refused to budge and threatened to try some of the hostages on a charge of spying on Iran for the USA.
- In April 1980, a rescue mission by US forces went horribly wrong in the Iranian desert. A helicopter and a refuelling aircraft collided in a staging area. Eight servicemen were killed and the operation was called off.
- Carter lost even more popularity because of his failure to secure the release of the hostages as well as the botched rescue attempt.

Negotiations for the release of the hostages resumed after the death of the Shah in July 1980. On 20 January 1981, 20 minutes after Reagan was sworn in as President, 52 American hostages were released by Iran into US custody, having spent 444 days in captivity.

▲ Figure 7.6: A map of the Middle East showing the main oil producing areas

> **Source J:** From a speech by the American President, Jimmy Carter, 7 April 1980, about the Iran hostage crisis
>
> We've made every effort to obtain their release on honorable, peaceful, and humanitarian terms, but the Iranians have refused to release them or even to improve the inhumane conditions under which these Americans are being held captive. I have today ordered the following steps.
>
> First, the United States of America is breaking diplomatic relations with the Government of Iran.
>
> Second, the Secretary of the Treasury will put into effect official sanctions prohibiting exports from the United States to Iran.
>
> I am committed to resolving this crisis. I am committed to the safe return of the American hostages and to the preservation of our national honor.

7 The search for world peace since 1970

◀ **Source K:** Iranian students massing outside the US Embassy in Tehran

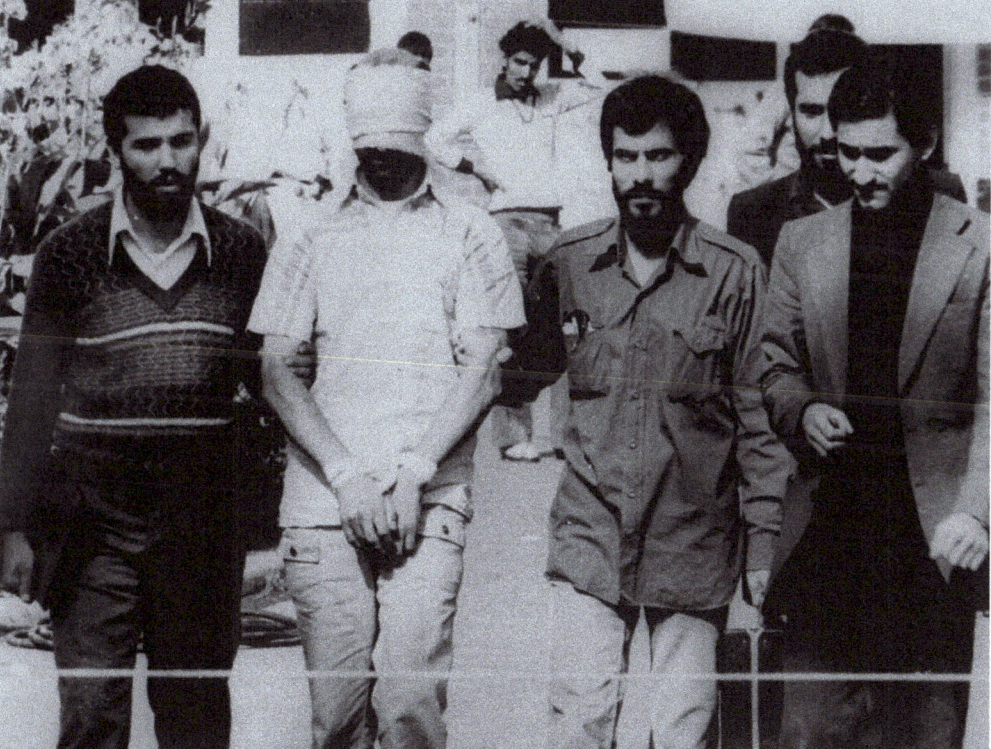

◀ **Source L:** One of the American hostages during the siege of the US Embassy

ACTIVITIES

1. What can you learn from Source J about American actions against Iran during the hostage crisis?
2. Working in pairs, put together two different captions for Source K:
   ☐ one for a US newspaper
   ☐ the other for an Iranian newspaper.
3. Source L was published in newspapers in the USA. What effects would this have had on American public opinion?

Practice question

Describe the events of the siege of the US Embassy in Tehran. *(For guidance, see page 108.)*

The Gulf War, 1990–91

On 2 August 1990 Saddam Hussein, the leader of Iraq, ordered the invasion of Kuwait, one of the leading oil producing countries in the Middle East. In less than 24 hours the country was under Iraqi control. Saddam invaded for several reasons.

- Burdened with debts from Iraq's war with Iran, Saddam saw Kuwait as a rich prize.
- Saddam claimed that Kuwait was historically part of Iraq, although in fact Kuwait had existed as a separate territory since 1899.
- Saddam did not expect the USA to use its military power in support of Kuwait. After all, the USA had been supporting him all the way through the war with the Iranian regime. He believed that the USA valued him as a stabilising influence within the region and in Iraq itself. They had taken no action against him when, in 1988, he brutally crushed a rebellion of the Kurds in the north of Iraq.

President Bush Snr took the lead in pressing for action to remove the Iraqis from Kuwait. He used the argument that it was an act of blatant aggression against a smaller neighbouring country. In reality, Bush wanted to protect US economic interests, especially oil interests, in the area (Source M).

> **Source M:** From George Bush Snr's address to Congress, 11 September 1990
>
> *So tonight, I want to talk to you about what's at stake – what we must do together to defend civilized values around the world and maintain our economic strength at home.*
>
> *Our objectives in the Persian Gulf are clear, our goals defined and familiar: Iraq must withdraw from Kuwait completely, immediately, and without condition. [Applause.] Kuwait's legitimate government must be restored. The security and stability of the Persian Gulf must be assured. And American citizens abroad must be protected. [Applause.]*

The United Nations imposed tough sanctions on Iraq and then the USA, Britain and other states sent forces to Saudi Arabia. This was called Operation Desert Shield, designed to defend Saudi Arabia and its vast oil resources from possible Iraqi attack as well as push Iraq out of Kuwait. In November 1990, the USA and its allies vastly increased their forces in the area.

Source N: US forces in Kuwait, 1991

Military campaigns

With almost 2,000 aircraft, General Norman Schwarzkopf, the US commander of the coalition forces in the Gulf, opened the campaign with an air assault. Operation Desert Storm, the air offensive against Iraq, was launched on 16 January 1991. In the first 10 hours a combination of stealth aircraft, cruise missiles, electronic warfare and precision-guided munitions took apart Iraq's military infrastructure and wrecked its ground forces.

After more than a month of 'softening up', Operation Desert Saber, the ground offensive to liberate Kuwait, was launched on 23 February 1991. By 27 February, Kuwait City had been taken by coalition troops and the following day the US ordered a ceasefire.

Outcome of the war

Saddam was allowed to withdraw with much of his army intact. The retreating Iraqis were at the mercy of the Allies, but Bush called a ceasefire because:

- he was afraid that if the slaughter continued, the allies would lose the support of the other Arab nations
- it was widely expected outside Iraq that, after his humiliating defeat, Saddam Hussein would soon be overthrown.

When the Gulf War ended in the defeat of Saddam, Bush's reputation stood high. However, as time passed, he was increasingly criticised for not having pressed home the advantage and for allowing the brutal Saddam to remain in power. Saddam not only survived but had enough troops, tanks and aircraft to brutally suppress rebellions by Shia Muslims in the south and the Kurds in the north.

Developments in foreign policy – conclusion

American foreign policy had undergone significant changes in the last 20 years of the twentieth century. Détente under Carter gave way to the 'Second Cold War' under Reagan. However, Gorbachev's reforms brought an end to the Cold War. The US became increasingly involved in the Middle East with the emergence of Islamic fundamentalism in Iran and the ambitions of the Iraqi dictator Saddam Hussein.

ACTIVITIES

1. What can you learn from Source M about the reasons the USA became involved in the Gulf War?
2. Put together a mind map to summarise the key features of the first Gulf War. Your mind map should include reasons for Saddam's invasion of Kuwait, US and world reactions, the defeat of Iraq and the results of the war.

Practice question

US foreign policy during the period 1970 to 1990 was influenced by developments such as:

- détente during the 1970s
- the Russian invasion of Afghanistan in 1979
- the friendship between Reagan and Gorbachev.

Arrange these events in order of their significance in influencing US foreign policy during this period. *(For guidance, see page 110–11.)*

Examination guidance

Examination Guidance for Question 1

This section provides guidance on how to answer a 'describe' question. Look at the following question.

> Describe the impact of the Wall Street Crash upon the US economy.

How to answer

1. Make sure you only include information which is directly relevant.
2. It is a good idea to start your answer using the words of the question. For example, 'The Wall Street Crash brought about dramatic change …'.
3. Try to include specific factual detail such as dates, events, names of key people.
4. Aim to write a good sized paragraph, covering at least three key features/points.

Example answer

Step One: Provide an opening statement which links to the question

> The Wall Street Crash of October 1929 brought about dramatic change to the US economy. The panic selling of shares which had begun on 19 October reached a peak on Black Thursday, 29 October, when over 13 million shares were sold and share prices collapsed.

Step Two: Build up support by including specific detail, covering a number of factors

> This sudden end to the boom period caused people to stop spending which in turn caused factories to reduce production and cut workers. Over the coming months and years millions of American people lost their jobs both in industry and farming. Unable to pay their rents, many lost their homes and were forced to move to temporary accommodation in shanty towns which were set up across American cities. They were nicknamed 'Hoovervilles' after the president who was criticised for doing little to help the growing number of unemployed. Others became hobos, hitching lifts on trains as they toured the countryside in search of work.

Step Three: End with a concluding sentence which links to the question

> The consequence of this was a sharp rise in unemployment which increased from 2.5 million at the end of 1929 to over 13 million by the end of 1932. Over 50% of black workers were unemployed. The US economy had gone from 'boom to bust' and the result was that America now entered a long period of economic slowdown known as the 'Great Depression' when there was little economic growth and unemployment remained very high. The Wall Street Crash therefore had a very dramatic impact upon the US economy for many years after 1929.

> **Now try the following question.**
> Describe Roosevelt's first New Deal.

Examination Guidance for Question 2

This section provides guidance on how to answer the 'how far' question. Look at the following question:

> How far did developments in music change the lives of young people in America during the 1950s and 1960s?

How to answer

1. You should aim to produce a well-supported judgement upon the extent of change.
2. You need to identify and discuss a number of factors to support your argument.
3. You must demonstrate good understanding of the topics under discussion.
4. Good factual detail will help to provide context.
5. End with concluding sentence which directly addresses the question.

Example answer

Step One: Provide an opening section which sets the scene

> Developments in music during the 1950s and 1960s did have a significant impact in influencing the lives of young American people. The 1950s witnessed the development of rock and roll music which was a style of music attractive to teenagers which was so very different from the music enjoyed by their parents.

Step Two: Identify and explain a number of factors, providing specific detail

> In 1956 Elvis Presley erupted onto the pop music scene and his songs such as 'Heartbreak Hotel' and 'Hound Dog' broke all sales records. Elvis was the first rock and roll star to influence the young in their attitude to authority and in their appearance. While parents disliked the new music and Elvis's sensual style of performing, together with his casual dress code, teenagers went out and copied his style. Many parents saw this as the beginning of the teenage rebellion which characterised the late 1950s and 1960s.

Step Three: Add additional factors, making reference to the degree of change

> During the 1960s the Beatles, the Rolling Stones and other British rock groups took America by storm, demonstrating the popularity and influence of pop music on American youth. The Beach Boys, a group formed in 1961, quickly emerged as a popular American rock band, whose dress and songs reflected the Southern California youth culture of cars, surfing and romance. To many middle class white parents such music appeared to breed teenage rebellion against authority and a lack of respect for the law. The 1960s also witnessed the development of the hippy movement and with it the music of protest which was used as a vehicle for anti-war and civil rights protest.

Step Four: End with a judgement which evaluates the degree of change

> While not all young American people became active followers of rock and roll, pop music and hippy culture, a large percentage did become influenced by these musical developments. For these young people music did have a significant influence in determining how they dressed, socialised, entertained themselves and generally how they lived their lives, playing a key role in what has been termed the age of 'teenage rebellion'. It was a very different lifestyle to that followed by their parents.

> **Now try the following question.**
> How far did the civil rights legislation of the early 1960s change the lives of black American people by 1970?

WJEC Eduqas GCSE History: The Development of the USA, 1929–2000

Examination Guidance for Question 3

This section provides guidance on how to answer the significance question. Look at the following question.

> Relations between the USA and USSR deteriorated between 1945 and 1963 due to events such as
> - The Truman Doctrine
> - The Berlin Blockade and airlift
> - The Cuban Missile Crisis.
>
> Arrange the developments in order of their significance in bringing about a deterioration in relations between the USA and USSR during this period. Explain your choices

How to answer

1. You need to decide in which order to write about the three factors – there is no correct order as it is the quality of the justification of your choice that is most important.
2. You need to demonstrate good subject knowledge by providing specific detail upon each factor.
3. You must fully explain the significance of each factor, using your knowledge to set them within their historical context.
4. Aim to provide a clear, well-supported justification for your reasoning.

Example answer

Step One: Provide an opening sentence which sets the scene

> The development of the Cold War after 1945 resulted in strained relations between the two superpowers, the USA and the USSR. A number of events between 1945 and 1963 served to strain this relationship to breaking point and by 1962 brought the two powers to the verge of a nuclear war.

Step Two: Select one factor and use your knowledge to discuss its significance

> One of the first incidents that strained the relationship was the launch of President Truman's Doctrine of Containment in 1947, which announced to the world a radical change in US foreign policy. Truman promised direct US involvement in the fight to stop the spread of communism and to contain it within its existing borders. He promised US support to any country threatened by communist aggression. It marked the beginnings of a policy of direct intervention and with it was the promise of financial aid in the form of the Marshall Plan. This seriously alarmed Stalin, the leader of the USSR, and he forbade the Communist countries of the Eastern block from accepting any financial aid. He viewed containment as a direct threat to the freedom of the USSR. Containment certainly added to the tension of the Cold War.

Examination guidance for the Eduqas Examination

Step Three: Select a second factor and use your knowledge to discuss its significance, making links to the other factors

> Another significant factor that served to cause a deterioration in the relationship between the USA and the USSR was the Berlin blockade and airlift of 1948–49. Fearful that West Berlin was being used as an escape route by those wishing to leave the Communist, East Stalin blocked off all road, rail and canal traffic to Berlin in an attempt to starve the Allies out of West Berlin. The West viewed Berlin as a test case and determined that the city would not fall to the communists. Applying the Containment theory, Truman decided to fly in supplies. The operation which started in June 1948 lasted ten months until Stalin called off the blockade in May 1949. America saw the operation as a success, proving that containment worked. Stalin grew ever more suspicious of the West. Relations between the two superpowers were strained further.

Step Four: Select a third factor and use your knowledge to discuss its significance, making links to the other factors

> The most significant cause of increased tension between the superpowers was over the Cuban Missile Crisis, an event which brought the world closest to a nuclear war. The Soviet decision to build missile launch sites on Cuba seriously worried the American President John F Kennedy. He decided that such missile sites posed a very serious threat to the security of the USA, and when it was discovered that nuclear headed missiles were being transported by ship across the Atlantic he ordered a quarantine zone around the island of Cuba, forbidding the Soviet ships from entering it. The result was a game of brinkmanship when the two most powerful nuclear powers pushed each other to the brink of war. In this instance the Soviets backed down and turned their ships around. The missiles did not get to Cuba.

Step Five: Conclude with a reasoned justification of your choice

> Of the three events, the Cuban Crisis was the most serious in that had the Soviets not backed down war could have been the result. The crisis strained the relationship between the superpowers but it also taught them the importance of not resorting to nuclear war. In many ways the Cuban Crisis was an outcome of the earlier conflicts over containment, one which threatened to turn the Cold War into a Hot War.

Now try the following question.

The lives of many American people changed between 1945 and the late 1960s due to the influence of developments such as:

- post-war affluence
- consumerism
- suburbanisation.

Arrange the developments in order of their significance in changing the lives of many American people between 1945 and the late 1960s. Explain your choices.

WJEC Eduqas GCSE History: The Development of the USA, 1929–2000

Examination Guidance for Question 4

This section provides advice on how to answer the 'explain why' question. Look at the following question.

> Explain why relations between the USA and China changed after 1970.

How to answer

1. 'Explain why' means to give reasons for something.
2. You need to provide a range of reasons.
3. Each reason needs to be supported with relevant factual detail.
4. Avoid generalised comments.
5. Make sure the information you include is directly relevant, that is, does it answer the question?

Example answer

Step One: Provide an opening sentence which sets the scene

> During the early 1970s relations between the superpowers improved as a result of a policy known as détente. This is a French word which was used to describe the relaxation of tension in the Cold War and one aspect of this policy was improved relations between the USA and China.

Step Two: Identify a reason why and use your knowledge to explain it

> During the late 1960s China's friendship with its fellow communist superpower, the USSR, began to breakdown, especially after China was critical of the Soviet invasion of Czechoslovakia in 1968. The new US president, Richard Nixon, had entered office with a pledge to end the war in Vietnam and he hoped to do this by becoming more friendly with China. As China was the chief supporter of the communist-led government in North Vietnam, Nixon hoped China could use its influence in helping to start peace negotiations. For its part, China hoped that improved relations with the USA would worry the USSR and serve to offset its declining relationship with the Soviets.

Step Three: Identify additional factors, remembering to include specific factual detail to explain them

> The desire for improved relations first began to emerge through sport. In April 1971 the US ping-pong team was invited to play in China and this helped to open up negotiations between the Chinese and American governments. The US wanted to improve trade links and in April 1971 lifted its 21-year-old trade embargo with China. Sport and trade helped to prepare the ground for improved political links. In February 1972 Nixon became the first US president to visit China when he went on a state visit to meet the communist leader, Mao Zedong. Both leaders hoped to gain from this meeting as it suited them both to build closer ties between their two countries.

Step Four: Conclude with a clear reference back to the question

> Nixon's visit changed Sino-US relations which had been cut for over two decades. It was a thawing of Cold War relations, a time which America and China entered a new era in their relationship. It also displayed a change in US foreign policy from one of open hostility to communist countries, to one of warmer, more friendly relations. This new friendship between the US and China occurred because it was advantageous to both sides. It was a period of détente in America's relationship with China.

Now try to answer the following question.

Explain why relations between the USA and Iran changed after 1979.

Examination Guidance for Question 5

This section provides guidance on how to answer the 'how important' question. Look at the following question.

> How important was the issue of education in the struggle for civil rights in the USA between 1941 and 1970?
>
> (In your answer you should discuss the importance of education alongside other factors in order to reach a judgement.)

How to answer

1. The question requires you to evaluate the importance or success of a particular event, movement or individual.
2. You must aim to analyse and evaluate the importance or significance of the factor named in the question.
3. You need to support your argument with specific factual detail.
4. You need to consider a counter-argument by considering the importance or significance of other factors.
5. You must end with a reasoned and well-supported judgement as to whether the factor named in the question was the most important factor.

Example answer

Step One: Refer to the key factor named in the question and outline its importance

> The issue of education was important in the struggle for civil rights in the USA for a number of reasons. One result of the Second World War was an increased awareness among the black community of the unfairness of segregation and during the 1950s and, with the help of the NAACP, a number of legal challenges were made to reverse the segregation laws. One of the most important areas of this challenge took place over the provision of education.

Step Two: Discuss the key factor in some detail, providing a judgement upon the degree of importance

> During the 1950s the NAACP led the fight against segregation in education. In 1954 the *Brown v. Board of Education of Topeka* case fought by the NAACP resulted in a landmark ruling by the Supreme Court which stated that segregation in education was illegal and therefore against the US Constitution. It was the first major success in the fight to end segregation, but as it was just a ruling and not a law many schools ignored it and continued to operate a segregated system of education. It took further action in the secondary sector before change took place. In 1957 nine black students attempted to exercise their legal right to attend the all-white Little Rock High School, but the Governor of Arkansas used the National Guard to prevent them from entering. It took President Eisenhower's decision to send 1,000 federal troops to Little Rock before the black students were allowed to attend school. Similarly, in 1962 President Kennedy had to send federal marshals to protect the black student James Meredith to exercise his right to attend Mississippi University. These changes in the primary, secondary and university sectors represented the first serious challenges to the segregation laws.

Step Three: Introduce other factors, using your knowledge to spell out their importance

The various campaigns to end segregation in education gained massive media attention, helping to raise the issue of civil rights across America. People began to realise how much could be achieved when black American people united and organised themselves. The fight in the educational field coincided and fuelled other developments at that time, such as the fight to end segregation on public transport. The Montgomery bus boycott of 1955–56 was a long legal battle which ultimately resulted in desegregation on the buses. It was an event which first brought Martin Luther King into the civil rights arena and it led to the formation of various civil rights groups such as the SCLC, the SNCC and CORE.

Step Four: Discuss other factors, evaluating their significance and importance

These organisations went on during the early 1960s to organise sit-in protests, freedom rides, marches and demonstrations in cities across the deep South such as Birmingham. The culmination of the marches was the march on Washington in August 1963 when Martin Luther King delivered his 'I have a dream' speech. Aside from these non-violent protests led by King was a more militant approach adopted by the likes of Malcolm X and Stokely Carmichael which led to the development of the Black Power movement. These campaigns kept the fight for civil rights in the media and raised awareness among US politicians that action was needed by the federal government.

Step Five: Conclusion – provide a reasoned judgement upon the degree of importance of the key factor when considered alongside other factors

The success of the *Brown v. Topeka* case was the catalyst which encouraged legal challenges against segregation in other areas such as transport. The Brown case proved that the courts could be used help fight for civil rights and the media attention it generated helped to turn public opinion and the opinion of the federal government against the injustices of segregation. The result was the passing of the Civil Rights Act 1964 and the Voting Rights Act 1965. The fight to secure change in educational provision was therefore very important in the fight to secure civil rights in the USA.

> **Now try the following question.**
>
> How important was Martin Luther King in the struggle for civil rights in the USA between 1941 and 1970?
>
> (In your answer you should discuss the importance of Martin Luther King alongside other factors in order to reach a judgement.)

Glossary

Air corridor   An air route along which aircraft are allowed to fly

Allied powers   Countries opposing Germany, Italy and Japan (Axis powers) during the Second World War, primarily Britain, France, USA and USSR

American Civil War   A war fought between the southern states (Confederacy) and the northern States, 1861–65

Anti-hero   Central character in a film who lacks the qualities of a normal hero

Baby boom   Temporary marked increase in the birth rate

Balance the budget   Ensure government spending matches revenue

Battle of the Bulge   Nickname for the Second Battle of the Ardennes, December 1944

Beatniks   Members of the Beat Generation

Berlin Wall   Wall built by the East Germans in 1961 to separate East and West Berlin

Blockade   The surrounding or blocking of a place

Bolshevik revolution   The seizure of power by the Bolsheviks (communists) in Russia in October 1917

Bonds   A certificate issued by the government promising to repay borrowed money

Brains trust   Later known as brain trust, this began as a term for a group of close advisors to a political candidate or incumbent, prized for their expertise in particular fields. The term is most associated with the group of advisors to Franklin Roosevelt during his presidential administration. More recently the use of the term has expanded to encompass any group of advisers to a decision maker, whether or not in politics

Brinkmanship   The policy of pushing a dangerous situation to the brink of disaster

Budget deficit   Overspending

Capitalism   Private ownership of the means of production

Civil rights   The rights of a citizen to social and political equality

Civil rights movement   The movement in the USA for equal rights for black citizens

Coalition forces   The countries who fought against Saddam Hussein during the first Gulf War

Cold War   State of hostility between the USA and the USSR without actual direct conflict, 1947–91

Collective bargaining   negotiation between workers, represented by union leaders, and employers

Communism   A political theory which advocates that all means of production should be owned by the state and each is paid according to his or her needs and abilities

Congress   The parliament of the USA divided into the Senate and the House of Representatives

Conscription   A law requiring all men or women of a certain age to join the armed forces

Constitutional   Actions which follow the constitutional system of government

Containment   The actions of the US government to prevent communism spreading to other countries

CORE   The Congress of Racial Equality, founded in 1942 to campaign for black civil rights

Counterculture   A way of life opposed to that which is regarded as normal

Coup d'etat   An armed revolution or uprising against an existing government

Defoliants   Chemicals sprayed on plants to remove their leaves. They were used by the US military to destroy the jungles of South Vietnam during the Vietnam War

Democrat   Supporter or member of the more reforming political party of the USA, the Democratic Party

Détente   An easing of strained relations

Direct action   Actions such as strikes or sit-ins

Disenfranchised   The loss of the right to vote

Dixiecrat   Member of the Democratic Party who opposed civil rights for black American people

Domino Theory   The belief that if one state fell to communism it would be quickly followed by neighbouring states

Drive-in cinema   A cinema where films could be watched while sitting in your car

Extradition   The official process whereby one nation or state surrenders a suspected or convicted criminal

FBI   The Federal Bureau of Investigation, set up to investigate organised crime

Feminist   Supporter of women's rights who believes that men and women are equal in all areas

Fireside chat   Radio talks given by President Roosevelt to keep up the morale of the American people

Freedom marches   Marches organised by Martin Luther King and others to campaign for civil rights

Freedom rides   These were taken by civil rights activists who rode interstate buses into the segregated southern United States to test the United States Supreme Court

Fundamentalist Someone who adheres strictly to the beliefs of a particular religion

General Motors A leading manufacturer of cars

Generation gap Difference in outlook and beliefs between members of two different generations

Great Depression The economic and social slump which followed the Wall Street Crash of 1929

Great Society The name given by President Johnson to his reforming programme of the 1960s

Gross national product The total value of all the final products and services produced in a given period by a country

Guerrilla A member of an irregular armed force that fights a stronger force by sabotage and harassment

Hobo An unemployed wanderer seeking work

Hooverville Shanty towns built on the edge of American cities by the unemployed during the early years of the Great Depression

House of Representatives The lower house of the US Congress

Impeachment To bring to trial for treason the president of the USA

Import duties Taxes on goods coming into the country

Indirect taxes A tax, such as a sales tax or value-added tax, that is levied on goods or services rather than individuals

Industrialist Someone who owns and/or runs a business

Infant mortality rate The number of deaths in the first year of life per 1,000 children born

Irangate Nickname given to a US political scandal in 1987 involving senior members of the Reagan administration

Iron Curtain Imaginary barrier to the passage of people and information between Soviet-controlled Eastern Europe and the West

Jim Crow Ethnic discrimination especially against black American people by legal enforcement

Ku Klux Klan Or KKK; a racist secret society of white people in the USA

Kurds An Iranian-speaking group who have historically inhabited the mountainous areas to the south of the Caucasus

Labour unions Trade unions in the USA

Laissez-faire The belief that people should help themselves rather than be helped by the state

Linkage Name given to Nixon's attempts to make links between various foreign policies, especially in Vietnam

Lynching The illegal execution, usually by hanging, of an accused person by a mob

Male supremacy The belief that society should be controlled by men

Method actors The name given to a genre of film actors who tried to think exactly like the character they were portraying

Montgomery Improvement Agency Or MIA; organisation set up to organise the Montgomery bus boycott

Migrate Move from one place to another

Militant Someone who holds extreme views and is prepared to use extreme, even violent, methods

Minimum wage The lowest legal wage per hour that someone can be paid

Multiplex movie theatre This is a cinema complex with more than three screens for viewing

Munitions Weapons of war

National Association for the Advancement of Colored People Or NAACP; organisation set up in 1909 to campaign for civil rights

National debt Money owed by the government

NATO North Atlantic Treaty Organisation set up in 1949, a defensive alliance of countries dominated by the USA

New Deal The name given to the policies of President Franklin Roosevelt to deal with the effects of the Great Depression

New Frontier The name given to the reform policies of President Kennedy in the early 1960s

Poll taxes A tax that was introduced in certain US states. This tax had to be paid before the person qualified for the vote

Reaganomics The nickname given to the economic policies of President Reagan

Recession This means a general slow-down in economic growth

Red Army The name given to the armed forces of the Soviet Union

Red Scare The name given to the growing fear of communism in the USA, especially in the years after the Second World War

Relief agencies Organisations set up to help those in poverty or the unemployed. More commonly associated with the New Deal, although Herbert Hoover also implemented some

Reparations Compensation paid to victorious countries for damage caused by defeated nations

Republican A member of one of the USA's more conservative political parties, the Republican Party

Rugged individualism The American ideal that individuals are responsible for their own lives without help from anyone else, especially the government

Segregation The enforced separation of racial groups in a community

Senate The upper house of the US Congress

Senator A representative from the upper house, the Senate. There are two senators per state

'Separate but equal' This was the legal justification in the USA for segregation, especially in education

Sexual permissiveness Freedom to have relationships outside marriage, often with more than one partner

Sharecropper A participant in a system of agriculture in which a landowner allows a tenant to use the land in return for a share of the crop produced on the land

Sit-ins A form of direct action that involves one or more persons non-violently occupying an area for a protest

Socialist Someone who believes that society as a whole should own the means of production, distribution and exchange

Southern Christian Leadership Conference Or SCLC; organisation set up in 1957 to campaign for civil rights for black American people

Soviet Union *see* USSR

State government Governments which are locally elected to run state affairs

State of the Union Address An annual address presented by the President of the United States to the United States Congress

Stock market A public market for the buying or selling of company shares

Student Non-violent Coordinating Committee Or SNCC; organisation set up in 1960 to campaign for black civil rights

Superpower A term used for the two most powerful countries in the world after 1945 – the USA and the USSR

Supreme Court The highest judicial body in the United States

Trade embargo A government banning trade with another country

Tupperware party A party organised to sell a range of plastic containers for storing food

United Nations An international organisation formed after the Second World War in 1945 to try to prevent wars and increase political and economic co-operation among member countries

Universal health insurance Health insurance which applies to all the population of a country

USSR Union of Soviet Socialist Republics, informally known as the Soviet Union, set up in 1924, broke up in 1991

Vietcong A communist guerrilla force that sought to overthrow the South Vietnamese government

Vietminh The League for the Independence of Vietnam, a nationalist- and communist-dominated movement

Vietnamisation The US government policy of transferring the fighting of the war in Vietnam from the American forces to those of South Vietnam

Wall Street Crash The term used for the collapse of the American stock market in October 1929

Warsaw Pact A military alliance set up in 1955 which included the Soviet Union and Eastern European states

Youth culture The beliefs, attitudes and interests of teenager

Index

AAA (Agricultural Adjustment Act) 14
affluence, post-war 23
Afghanistan 97-8
African-American 24
    see also civil rights
Agricultural Adjustment Act (AAA) 14
Alphabet Agencies 14, 17, 18
American Liberty League 18
anti-war protests 74-5
arms race 101
automobile industry 22

baby boom 24
Bay of Pigs invasion 87
'Beat Generation' 71
Berlin Crises
    1948-49 84-5
    1961 86
Berlin Wall 86, 100, 103
Birmingham March 41
black American 17, 24, 25
    see also civil rights
Black Muslims 44, 45
Black Panther movement 52-3
Black Power movement 50-1
Bonus Marchers 9
Brezhnev, Leonid 94
Brown v. *Topeka* 31-2
budget deficit 61, 63, 64
Bush, George H. 63, 101, 106, 107

Carmichael, Stokely 44, 50
Carter, Jimmy 61, 98
Castro, Fidel 87-8
CCC (Civilian Conservation Corps) 14, 15
China 96
cinema 68
civil rights
    Black Panther movement 52-3
    Black Power movement 50-1
    education 31-4
    freedom riders 39
    legislation 46-8
    Malcolm X 44-5
    Martin Luther King 40-3
    Montgomery bus boycott 35-7
    race riots 29, 49
    and Reagan 62
    Second World War 26-30
    sit-ins 29, 38
    and students 74
Civil Rights Act (1964) 46, 56
Civil Works Administration (CWA) 14
Civilian Conservation Corps (CCC) 14, 15
Clinton, Bill 64-5
Cold War
    Berlin crisis 84-6

Cuban Missile crisis 87-8
defence spending 22
end of 102-3
industry 23
Truman doctrine 82-3
US involvement 80-1
communism 80-1, 100, 102-3
computer industry 22, 70
Congress of Racial Equality (CORE) 29, 39, 42
Connor, Eugene 'Bull' 39, 41
consumerism 23
CORE (Congress of Racial Equality) 29, 39, 42
Coughlin, Charles 18
counterculture 71
Cuban Missile crisis 87-8
CWA (Civil Works Administration) 14
Czechoslovakia 94, 96, 102
    see also satellite states

defence spending 22, 61
Democrats 18
détente 94-5
discrimination 17, 78
    see also civil rights
Domino Theory 83
drugs
    taking 73
    war on 62, 63

EBA (Emergency Banking Act) 14
economic downturn
    Great Depression 6-9
    Wall Street Crash 6
education, and black Americans 31-4
Eisenhower, Dwight D. 23, 27, 33
Emergency Banking Act (EBA) 14
environment policies 62, 63
Equal Pay Act 79

Fair Deal programme 30
Fair Employment Practices Commission (FEPC) 28
Fair Labour Standards Act 16
Farm Credit Administration (FCA) 14
farming
    Great Depression 7
    Hoover's policies 10
FCA (Farm Credit Administration) 14
Federal Emergency Relief Administration (FERA) 14
feminists 79
FEPC (Fair Employment Practices Commission) 28
FERA (Federal Emergency Relief Administration) 14

fireside chats (Roosevelt) 13, 15
freedom riders 39
Friedan, Betty 71, 78

Gates, Bill 70
Gorbachev, Mikhail 100-3
Great Depression 6-9
Great Society 56-7, 92
Gulf War (1990-91) 106-7

health care 25, 56, 61, 64
Helsinki Agreements 95
hippy movement 73
HIV/AIDS 62
Hoover, Herbert 10-11, 12
Hoovervilles 7, 8
house building 22

industry
    after Second World War 22
    Second World War 20-1
infant mortality rate 64
information technology 70
infrastructure 17
Intermediate Nuclear Forces (INF) Treaty 101
internet 70
Iran 104-5
Iranian hostages 104-5
Iraq 106-7

James Meredith case 34
Jay-Z 67
Jim Crow army 26
Jim Crow laws 31
Johnson, Lyndon 43, 46, 47-8, 56-7, 92

Kennan, George 81
Kennedy, John F.
    Berlin crisis (1961) 86
    and civil rights 39, 41, 43
    Cuban Missile crisis 87-8
    domestic policies 54-5
    New Frontier 54-5
Kerner report 49
Khrushchev, Nikita 86, 87-8
King, Martin Luther 36, 37, 40-3
Kissinger, Henry 92
Korean War 23
Kuwait 106-7

Lend Lease programme 20
Lewinsky, Monica 65
literature 71
Little Rock High School 33-4
Long, Huey 18
Long Telegram 81

118

Malcolm X 44-5
Marshall Plan 83
Marshall, Thurgood 31, 44, 55
McCarthyism 80
medical care 25, 56, 61
Mexico Olympics 51
MIA (Montgomery Improvement Association) 36
Microsoft 70
Montgomery bus boycott 35-7
Montgomery Improvement Association (MIA) 36
Moscow summit 101
music 66-7

NAACP (National Association for the Advancement of Coloured People) 29, 30, 42
Nation of Islam 44
National Association for the Advancement of Coloured People (NAACP) 29, 30, 42
national debt 61, 63
National Labour Relations Act (Wagner Act) 16, 18
National Organisation for Women (NOW) 78
National Recovery Administration (NRA) 14, 17
NATO (North Atlantic Treaty Organisation) 84, 85-6
New Deal 13, 16-19
New Frontier 54-5
Newton, Huey 52
Nixon Doctrine 93
Nixon, Richard 58-60, 75, 92, 93, 94
North Atlantic Treaty Organisation (NATO)
    see NATO (North Atlantic Treaty Organisation)
NOW (National Organisation for Women) 78
NRA (National Recovery Administration) 14, 17
nuclear weapons testing 88

Operation Desert Shield 106
Operation Rolling Thunder 90

Parks, Rosa 35, 36, 37
perestroika (restructuring) 100
Perkins, Frances 13, 17
personal computers 70
ping-pong diplomacy 96
Plessy v. *Ferguson* case 31
Poland 81, 102
    see also satellite states
Potsdam Conference 81
Presley, Elvis 66
protest singers 74
Public Works Administration (PWA) 14

race riots 29, 49, 63
racism 26-7
    see also civil rights

Randolph, A. Philip 28, 42
Reagan, Ronald 61-2, 99, 100-1
'Reaganomics' 61
Reconstruction Finance Corporation (RFC) 14
Red Scare 80
relief agencies 10
reparations 81
Republican policies
    Great Depression 10-11
    New Deal 18
RFC (Reconstruction Finance Corporation) 14
riots 29, 49, 63
rock and roll music 66
Roosevelt, Eleanor 17, 78
Roosevelt, Franklin D.
    1932 presidential election 12
    Alphabet Agencies 14
    death 23
    discrimination policies 28
    New Deal 13
    second New Deal 15-19
rugged individualism 10

Saddam Hussein 106-7
SALT agreements 95
satellite states 80, 100, 102, 103
scandals, and Clinton 65
SCLC (Southern Christian Leadership Conference) 39, 40, 42
SDI (Strategic Defence Initiative) 99
SDS (Students for a Democratic Society) 74
Seale, Bobby 52
Second Cold War 99
second New Deal 16-19
Second World War
    and black American people 26-30
    impact on women 76
    industrial output 20-1
segregation 17, 31
    see also civil rights
Selma, Alabama 43
Selma march 47-8
'Sick Chickens' case 19
sit-ins 29, 38
SNCC (Student Non-violent Coordinating Committee) 39, 42, 50
Social Security Act 16, 17, 19
social welfare 16, 17
Southern Christian Leadership Conference (SCLC) 39, 40, 42
Soviet satellite states 80, 100, 102, 103
space programme 62
Stalin, Joseph 80-1, 83, 84-6
standard of living 23
'Star Wars' programme 99
START (Strategic Arms Limitation) 101
stock market crashes
    (1929) 6
    (1987) 61

Strategic Arms Limitation (START) 101
Strategic Defence Initiative (SDI) 99
Student Non-violent Coordinating Committee (SNCC) 39, 50
student protests 74-5
Students for a Democratic Society (SDS) 74
Supreme Court, and New Deal 18

television 23, 69
Tennessee Valley Authority (TVA) 14, 20
Townsend, Francis 18
Truman Doctrine 82-3
Truman, Harry S. 23, 29, 30, 80-1
TVA (Tennessee Valley Authority) 14, 20

unemployment 17, 64
    Great Depression 7-8, 11
    and New Deal 17
    and Second World War 20-1
US military, and black American people 26-7
US production, scale of 21
US v. *Butler* case 19
USSR
    and Afghanistan 97-8
    Cold War 80-1
    collapse of 102-3
    and Czechoslovakia 94
    and NATO 85-6
    and Warsaw Pact 86

Vietnam peace talks 92
Vietnam War 57, 74, 89-93
Voter Education Project 47
voting rights 47-8
Voting Rights Act (1965) 48, 56

Wagner Act (National Labour Relations Act) 16, 18
Wall Street Crash 6
War Production Board (WPB) 20, 21
Warsaw Pact 86
Washington march 42-3
Watergate scandal 58-60
welfare services 25, 55, 56, 61, 64
Whitewater scandal 65
women
    changing role of 76-9
    isolation 24
    and literature 71
    and New Deal 17
    and Second World War 21
Women's Liberation Movement 71, 79
women's rights 78
Woodstock rock concert 73
Works Progress Administration (WPA) 16
WPB (War Production Board) 21

Yalta Conference 81
Yeltsin, Boris 103
youth counterculture 73
youth culture 67, 72, 75

Acknowledgements

The Publishers would like to thank the following for permission to reproduce copyright material:

Photo credits: p.7 © The Granger Collection/TopFoto; **p.8** © 2000 Credit: Topham/AP; p.9 © Bettmann/Getty Images; **p.11** © Granger, NYC/Alamy Stock Photo; **p.12** 'Smilette', Democrat Election Poster, 1932 (litho), American School, (20th century)/Private Collection/Peter Newark American Pictures/Bridgeman Images; **p.15** t © Franklin D. Roosevelt Library; b © MPI/Getty Images; **p.19** © Punch Limited; **p.22** © Bettmann/Getty Images; **p.23** © Mary Evans Picture Library; **p.24** © Bettmann/Contributor/Getty Images; **p.25** © Andreas Feininger/The LIFE Picture Collection/Getty Images; **p.27** The U.S. National Archives,111-SC-337901; **p.28** Courtesy of the Library of Congress, LC-USW3-034282-C; **p.29** © Bettmann/Contributor/Getty Images; **p.32** © AP/Press Association Images; **p.33** © Bettmann/Contributor/Getty Images; **p.35** ©The Image Works/TopFoto; **p.36** © Don Cravens/The LIFE Images Collection/Getty Images; **p.37** © Don Cravens/The LIFE Images Collection/Getty Images; **p.38** © Granger, NYC/Alamy Stock Photo; **p.40** © Everett Collection/REX/Shutterstock. **p.41** ©2000 Credit:Topham/AP; **p.42** © Agence France Presse/Contributor/Getty Images; **p.44** © Bettmann/Contributor/Getty Images; **p.46** LBJ Library photo by Cecil Stoughton; **p.47** © Bettmann/Contributor/Getty Images; **p.49** © Bettmann/Contributor/Getty Images; **p.50** © Flip Schulke/Corbis/Getty Images; **p.51** © Rolls Press/Popperfoto/Contributor/Getty Images; **p.52** © Bettmann/Contributor/Getty Images; **p.53** © David J. & Janice L. Frent/Corbis/Getty Images; **p.55** © Everett Collection Historical/Alamy Stock Photo; **p.57** t © Punch Ltd; b © Everett Collection Historical/Alamy Stock Photo; **p.58** A 1973 Herblock Cartoon, © The Herb Block Foundation; **p.61** © Bettmann/Getty Images; **p.62** © Act Up AIDS/Alamy Stock Photo; **p.63** © Fotosearch/Getty Images; **p.65** © Juana Arias/The Washington Post/Getty Images; **p.66** © Bettmann/Contributor/Getty Images; **p.67** l © Michael Ochs Archives/Getty Images; r © Mitchell Gerber/Corbis/VCG/Getty Images; **p.69** © Everett Collection/REX/Shutterstock; **p.70** © Division of Medicine & Science, National Museum of American History, Smithsonian Institution; **p.72** © Everett Collection/REX/Shutterstock; **p.73** © Bettmann/Contributor/Getty Images; **p.75** © Bettmann/Contributor/Getty Images; **p.76** The U.S. National Archives, NWDNS-179-WP-1563; **p.77** © Bettmann/Contributor/Getty Images; **p.82** Courtesy of the Harry S. Truman Library, Independence, Missouri; **p.83** © Bettmann/Contributor/Getty Images; **p.85** © Punch Ltd; **p.86** ©2003 TopFoto; **p.90** © AP/Press Association Images; **p.91** ©2000 TopFoto; **p.92** © Bettmann/Contributor/Getty Images; **p.93** © Lee Snider/Getty Images; **p.95** © Bettmann/Contributor/Getty Images; **p.96** © Bettmann/Contributor/Getty Images; **p.97** © TASS/TopFoto; **p.101** © Peter Heimsath/REX/Shutterstock; **p.105** t © Sipa Press/REX/Shutterstock; b © AP/Press Association Images; **p.106** © John Gaps III/AP/Press Association.

Text acknowledgements

p.9 Source F: A.E. McIntyre, quoted in J. Simkin from Evidence and Empathy: America in the Twenties, 1986; **p.13** Source I: Address Of The President Delivered By Radio From The White House. Monday, July 24, 1933; **p.21** Table 2.2: Milward, Alan S. War, Economy, and Society, 1939-1945. **p.69** Berkeley: University of California Press, 1979; **p.61** Source F: Ronald Reagan, quoted in Harriet Ward, World Powers (1985); **p.81** Source C: Republished with permission of Foreign Affairs, from Sources of Soviet conduct, George Frost Kennan, 1947; permission conveyed through Copyright Clearance Center, Inc.; **p.90** Source J: A Bright Shining Lie by Neil Sheehan, published by Modern Library. Reprinted by permission of The Random House Group Limited; **p.91** Source M: James R. Ebert, A Life in a Year: The American Infantryman in Vietnam, 1965-1972, Presidio Press, 1995; **p.104** Source J: Jimmy Carter, Sanctions Against Iran Remarks Announcing US Actions, April 7, 1980.

Every effort has been made to trace all copyright holders, but if any have been inadvertently overlooked, the Publishers will be pleased to make the necessary arrangements at the first opportunity.